MW01032286

HEAVEN

ON

EARTH

UNVEILING THE MYSTERY OF
GOD'S KINGDOM

DR. JIM RICHARDS

True Potential
REACH THE WORLD

Copyright © 2018 Dr. Jim Richards

All rights reserved.

No part of this publication may be reproduced, stored, or transmitted in any form or by any means, including written, copied, or electronically, without prior written permission from the author or his agents. The only exception is brief quotations in printed reviews. Short excerpts may be used with the publisher's or author's expressed written permission.

All Scripture quotations, unless otherwise noted are from the King James Version of the Bible.

Heaven on Earth: Unveiling the Mystery of God's Kingdom

Cover and Interior Page design by True Potential, Inc.

ISBN: (paperback): 9781948794367
ISBN: (ebook): 9781948794374

True Potential, Inc.
PO Box 904, Travelers Rest, SC 29690
www.truepotentialmedia.com

Produced and Printed in the United States of America.

Table of Contents

Start Here!

Intention changes what the mind sees and the heart perceives. For you to engage your intention, it is essential that you know the purpose of this book before you begin. Please read this page and before you begin reading make a determination: I agree with the stated purposes of this book. I am open to the Holy Spirit to show me what I need to see, perceive and understand.

The goal: Experiencing The Abundant life!

Jesus said He came to give us the abundant life. The Greek word for life is "zoe." Its literal meaning is: *the quality of life possessed by the one who gives it*! In other words, Jesus wants us to have the same quality of life He is experiencing with God!

This book has one very simple purpose! I want to give you the information and the tools needed to experience the very best quality of life possible, while you are on planet earth: the abundant life.

The Problem: Not knowing, trusting and follow Jesus' teachings!

Much of the complication and frustration for the believer in pursuing this life, is religion has taken us off course. We are pursuing what God is offering, but we are not pursuing it as Jesus instructed. Words have been redefined to mean something completely different than the original intention. Customs and colloquialisms of the time are completely ignored when interpreting His teachings. The Bible is not used to translate the Bible: the Scriptures that provide types and symbols are not used. But the most egregious negligence of Bible interpretation is the death, burial, and resurrection of Jesus, i.e. the basis of the New Covenant!

Jesus taught us how to experience heaven on earth. It's actually pretty straightforward. He called it the Kingdom of God. There's nothing complicated about it. This book is written, based on Jesus' teaching, to unravel the Mystery of the Kingdom.

We Are the Body oF Christ

Rom. 12: 4-5

1 Corth 12:12-13

1 " 10:16-17

1 " 3-16

Intention Statement:

I intend to live the abundant life! I will read this material with an open mind, remaining loyal to the scripture, while allowing the Holy Spirit to be my personal teacher! I desire to live, move and have my being in the realm Jesus called the Kingdom of God, and enjoy all the associated benefits!

CHAPTER 1

The Problem with the Promise

The greatest deception is not an outright lie, but a partial truth coupled with a lie.

Jesus was born in the exact year the prophet Daniel had predicted. It was this prophetic knowledge that caused Herod and much of Israel to be hyper-attentive. They had a clear understanding of the times. Among those who knew what to expect, there was great anticipation, most of which was based on partial truth. The human tendency to accept portions of God's Word as it is stated while twisting others to fit our personal preferences is called ***mixed motives.*** 2 Peter 3: 16

Mixed motives may be the most difficult of all mindsets from which to ever gain clarity or freedom. When based on mixed motives, any time a belief or action is called into question, we point to the biblical aspect of the belief to validate its legitimacy. All we need is a small amount of truth to justify an entirely false concept and blind ourselves to the fact that it is false. Although not consciously, we deliberately make destructive choices daily, in every arena of life, to soothe our conscience. Like politicians pushing a corrupt agenda by pointing to one small positive benefit, all the harm is hidden in the one positive benefit.

The result, tragically, is that a mixed motive corrupts the entirety of the fruit it produces. God warned that a little leaven leavens the entire loaf. When corrupt motives are justified by partial truths, we are blinded more than when we believe a complete lie. The leaders of Israel were corrupt; they may have understood many of the prophecies of the coming of Messiah, but they were not interested in God fulfilling His purposes in the earth. They wanted the Messiah to fulfill their purposes. They believed for a Messiah who would fulfill their corrupt, selfish intentions, much like believers who long for a salvation to merely fulfill their lusts and personal ambitions.

An innate deception stands in direct opposition to all that is true, healthy, and life-giving. In other words, for every truth, there is potential for a specific deception. The Hebrew language is very clear that all truth possesses a light side and a dark side. The way we interpret any truth is determined by whether we decide if that truth will bring us life or death. For example, the word that God gave to Moses brought life and freedom to the children of Israel, but it brought death to the Egyptians. Every Word of God has the potential for life or death. The misinterpretation, then, does not stem from the Word; it stems from our heart. The *heart* is the core of our beliefs. When we do not believe God is who He says He is, our interpretation of scripture brings fear, unbelief, and death. Conversely, when we believe God's character is consistent with His names and the life of Jesus, every word brings life.

God has actually provided clear processes for making our lives incredibly rich with peace, joy and overall quality of life. Many people believe God wants them to have an abundant life, but a biblically-based belief mixed with an unbiblical application is a recipe for conflict and pain. One of the laws of the Kingdom is the law of the seed, and its second principle teaches: "By planting discordant seeds with the Word of God, we corrupt the seed of God's Word, and the crop it produces is contaminated!"

In our pursuit of the happiness Jesus undeniably guarantees, we mix the promise with a corrupt, anti-biblical seed that infers others must change for us to be happy. From this corrupt logic, we impose our will onto others demanding that they make us happy, justifying it with a biblical promise. So deep is this rotting selfishness that we even demand God be who we want Him to be and His salvation be as we think it should be. In actuality, we want a god created in our image to fulfill our will. This corrupt selfishness opposes the Lordship of Jesus and the unchangeable nature of God. From a mixed motive of the promised abundant life and a selfish agenda, the seed of God's Word is destroyed and its harvest produces more pain and unhappiness.

All the kings of the ancient world knew a Deliverer would one day come to restore man to God and planet earth to the perfect will of God, as demonstrated in the Garden of Eden. This, in fact, was the first recorded prophecy of the Bible, spoken by God Himself in the Garden of Eden, "a deliverer, born of a woman, would overthrow the power of Lucifer and the kingdoms of this world"[1] The godless feared that when this prophecy was fulfilled they would lose their kingdoms, power, wealth and rule over men. Throughout ancient history, counterfeit fulfillments of this prophecy were staged as a means to seduce the human race into giving their allegiance to corrupt men and women of power. The Bible reveals

1　　Gen. 3:15, "And I will put enmity between you and the woman, And between your seed and her Seed; He shall bruise your head, And you shall bruise His heel." (NKJV)

that with any known sign of an emerging deliverer, mass murders and atrocities were committed to protect the power of evil rulers and their empires.

Sadly, even the Jews who longed for the Messiah's arrival had taken themselves into such a state of *selective processing*,[1] they would not accept what the Scripture clearly revealed: "The Messiah would appear twice; first, as a suffering servant and second, as a ruling King." They wanted the Lion of the tribe of Judah and had no interest in the Lamb who would take away the sins of the world. They were so convinced of what they needed to be happy and free, that even when Jesus proved beyond any doubt that He was who He claimed to be, they killed Him. In fact, had He not so irrefutably proven Himself to be the Messiah by the evidence they demanded, they could have disqualified Him. Nevertheless, by fulfilling what they had determined were miracles that could only be done by the Messiah, they had to either kill Him or acknowledge Him.

Imagine the extreme internal reactions experienced by both groups when John the Baptist announced that the ***Kingdom of God*** was at hand. The Jews became hopeful, even ecstatic at the possibility of finally breaking the power of the Romans; they must have reveled in their retaliatory fantasies for every oppressive, crooked action taken against them. Surely their vengeance exploded from hot embers into flame at the notion of finally conquering their mortal enemy. Even more intoxicating was the supposition that Israel would rule all the nations of the world alongside the Messiah.

The ruling class, on the other hand, feared losing their positions of power and wealth. They did not want a kingdom where God ruled; they wanted a kingdom they ruled. The wicked rulers had already attempted to prevent the advent of the Messiah by killing all the newborn male babies at the time of Christ's birth, just as Nimrod did at the sign of Abraham's birth. They were poised for extreme ruthless action to secure their control. Murder, destruction, and oppression are always justified by those who believe the end justifies the means. Like Pharaoh, the promise of the Deliverer was wholly anticipated by the people but highly dreaded by the rulers.

When Jesus came preaching the Kingdom of God, the corrupted Jewish leaders thought He was referring to world domination; it was everything they had hoped. Conversely, the godless religious leaders felt their greatest fear had come to pass. By this time, the high priests and rulers of Israel were being appointed by Rome, positions they usually obtained by paying bribes, not positions intended to serve the people of Israel but for the power to benefit themselves and administer their corrupt agendas, at the will of Rome.

The common people had few agendas: they simply wanted a better quality of life and to know God. Throughout history, many have misunderstood that it

---

1   **Selective processing** occurs when a person's desires, prejudices, or judgments cause them to only perceive that which supports their position.

was not the common people of Israel who killed Jesus. It was, as it always has been and always will be, corrupt politicians who thrive on power and control who killed the Savior of the world. Jesus did not fulfill the political ambitions of those Jews with mixed motives. As the people began to follow Him, He quickly became a threat to the authority and control of the corrupt religious and political administration. Pagan rulers feared the wrath of Rome and the loss of position and power, even possible punishment. To them, Jesus most certainly did not fit the Kingly profile of those who craved power and position. Even among the religious leaders, He was a threat to *their ministry*.

The problem with the promise is understood by one question Jesus poses, "What does the scripture say and how do you read it?" The problem is never whether or not the promise is clear: the promise is always clear. We complicate the promise through our unbelief and/or our personal agendas. Corrupt seed destroys our capacity to see the obvious and hear that which has been clearly stated.

HeartWork[1]

Read This Aloud Before Every HeartWork Session: The Kingdom of God is internal. HeartWork is designed to remove any internal obstacles that prevent me from entering the realm where I experience Heaven on Earth.

Read the following questions and prepare yourself to see and perceive, to hear and understand. Be honest about the beliefs or agendas that will prevent you from hearing and receiving God's promises.

1. I have some personal goals or agendas that I have to make happen. Therefore, I fear putting them in God's hands.

2. When my understanding of scripture is challenged or questioned, I feel threatened.

3. I really believe I can only have happiness if certain people do what I need them to do.

4. I am willing to surrender all my opinions and interpretations when I see it in the Word.

5. I trust the Word of God and the Holy Spirit to be my teacher.

---

1   HeartWork is a term used in Heart Physics that explains the biblical process for influencing our heart and changing our beliefs.

CHAPTER 2

The Gospel of the Kingdom

The clearest expression of faith is a humble heart.

Jesus was a teacher of the *Kingdom of God*, commonly referred to as the **Kingdom of Heaven**. Simply hearing the phrase *Kingdom of God* evoked all manner of thoughts and emotions in all manner of people. Hearers either interpreted Jesus's teaching based on their predetermined opinions and personal desires or they allowed their hearts to remain open to being taught of the Lord.

Only those who had no lust for power - just the passion to know God and have a better quality of life - grasped and benefited from His Kingdom teaching. Today's believers are as unclear about Jesus' Kingdom teaching as those who heard it firsthand. Our intention to find happiness from that which occurs in the natural stands in complete opposition to His teaching. As the cornerstone parable of the Kingdom, the parable of the sower and the seed never indicates that anything outside of us must change in order to enter into the Kingdom realm. It clearly illustrates the factors that determine whether or not the seed (Word) is sown in the soil of our heart and survives long enough to bear fruit.

Jesus encapsulated our tendency to selectively process information when He said, *"Hearing you will hear and shall not understand, and seeing you will see and not perceive."* (Matthew 13:14) Some believe that God closed people's eyes and ears, but He clarifies this in verse 15, "For the hearts of this people have grown dull. Their ears are hard of hearing." He is describing an issue of the heart, a **hardness or blindness of heart**. Our heart is the means by which God communicates with us. We and we alone have dominion over our hearts, its attitudes and beliefs, which determine our softness or hardness toward God. A hard heart is insensitive and even resistant to God. The seed that fell on the hard soil was the seed that was lost most quickly.

As Jesus continues in the same verse, it becomes evident that it is we who choose to close our eyes and ears, *"And their eyes they have closed, Lest they should see with their eyes and hear with their ears."* God never arbitrarily decides who will believe and who will not, who will rebel and who will surrender. He desires for all men to come to the knowledge of the truth. Each of us, individually, opens and closes our heart to God based on our knowledge and trust for His character and His Word, and our willingness to give up our personal agendas. When God is not who we want him to be, we often create a false image of God. When His Word does not say what we want it to say we create a corrupt interpretation of His Word. We read the Word intending to see what our heart desires.

The key to understanding this passage (verse 15) is found in the statement, "Lest they should understand with their hearts and turn." It is impossible to understand God's truth when attempting to make it fit into our own logic. If the only way we can feel happy, safe or fulfilled is based on our predetermined opinion, any other point of view is illogical and incomprehensible. Upon determining what we want to see, we selectively process out that which differs from our established view. We never see it. This is why Jesus asked, *"What is written in the law and how do you read it?"*[1] No one ever just reads the Bible; we read *and* interpret it. Many external sources are available to use as a basis for interpretation, but truth can only be grasped by the **humble** (teachable).

To turn to God in surrender of our opinion is more than accepting a single truth or fact; it is accepting a logical thought process that is foreign to ours, even though ours is the one we trust. The willingness to surrender our opinion to His is one of the clearest expressions of faith in God. That faith, however, becomes an impossibility every time we believe the only path to happiness, pleasure or fulfillment is for things to happen our way, according to our plan.

Until we understand exactly what Jesus meant by the phrase *Kingdom of God*, we remain in darkness concerning His central message. Jesus came proclaiming the message of the Kingdom; it is the message of the Kingdom that must be preached to the ends of the earth before He can return, yet we seem to know less about His Kingdom than any other aspect of our doctrine.

The problem with the promise is seldom the inability to see the promise. The problem with the promise is that our idea of how that promise will be fulfilled in us is usually twisted into a theological premise based on our personal preference or opinion. God's Word always shows us the process for experiencing the promise; our inability to understand that process is the abyss of our personal opinion.

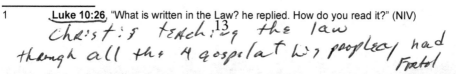

1   Luke 10:26, "What is written in the Law? he replied. How do you read it?" (NIV)

13

Christ is teaching the law through all the 4 gospel at his prophecy had Foetol

This book, *Heaven on Earth,* will not only help us to understand the message of the Kingdom clearly, but it will explicitly show us what Jesus taught about how to establish our lives in the Kingdom. It is, therefore, paramount to prepare ourselves to see, hear and understand truth in a context that will most likely violate our personal logic. *Body of Christ (ey Rom 16:25 a NEW (way to Christ gRACE*

Being teachable (humble) is simply a choice, 50% decision and 50% faith. The decision to open our hearts to God to make a journey we have never made, to follow a wisdom we have never acquired, to experience a quality of life we have never seen, must be made by trusting Him to lead, guide, protect and teach us every step of the way. Commitment to His Lordship is the only path by which we can follow Him as a disciple and enter into this internal realm called the Kingdom of God!

HeartWork

Read This Aloud Before Every HeartWork Session: The Kingdom of God is internal. HeartWork is designed to remove any internal obstacles that prevent me from entering the realm where I experience Heaven on Earth!

Before moving ahead to the next chapter, prepare yourself by participating in *A Mentoring Moment*. Answer these questions honestly. Do not answer them as you feel you should; answer them based on what is really in your heart.

1. If understanding the message of the *Kingdom* means I will have to surrender long-held beliefs and opinions to scriptural truth, am I willing to do so?

2. Do I feel the need to protect the doctrines held by my parents, people I respect or my denomination?

3. Am I able to value the input of others even when I realize not all of their input is accurate?

CHAPTER 3

Discovering the Door to the Kingdom

The Kingdom of God is only accessible through the door of the heart!

John the Baptist appeared proclaiming, *"Repent, for the Kingdom of heaven is at hand."* (Matt. 3:2, ESV) Jesus soon followed, preaching, *"The Kingdom is at hand!"* **Carnal** religious minds imagined the fulfillment of all their ideas and aspirations of the Kingdom of God coming to earth, but the Kingdom never manifested to their liking. Perhaps one of the many reasons they would cease to follow Jesus was because he was not producing the Kingdom they wanted. *it has not come yet! I w*

It could be argued that the Jewish people had an excuse. How were they to know Jesus would establish God's Kingdom in phases? It would be internal at His first appearing, then external, in the world, at His second coming, and finally, in its ultimate expression, when New Jerusalem comes to planet earth and abides forever. Likewise, many could argue that upon hearing the Gospel today we cannot be expected to grasp the mysteries of the Kingdom either. More often than not, these arguments are actually a form of internal and sometimes subconscious resistance to a message contrary to our predetermined beliefs. *it will in th 1000 yr*

The truth, however, is just the opposite. As we will soon discover, there were very distinct choices made by some listeners which made it possible for them to discover the door that led to the understanding of all the mysteries of the Kingdom. It started with John preaching the message of repentance as the key component to internal preparation for the soon coming Kingdom of God. **Repentance**, in its most basic form, means: *to have a change of mind.* We could generalize the many things about which we must change our minds, but at this point, *a change* *of mind* is all we need to understand about repentance.

The Messiah, for which they had prayed and waited, was about to be revealed, and He would teach them all they needed to know to enter the Kingdom of God and of Heaven. In other words, if they had any intention of being disciples of the Messiah, they had to repent of the obvious or repent (change their beliefs) when His teaching conflicted with any of their currently held doctrine, tradition, view, or opinion about life or God. Repentance is the attitude of the teachable who are ready to surrender their closely held opinions when presented with a truth clearly supported by scripture.

The Kingdom of God is called a **mystery**. Like most of the mysteries of God, they are hidden in plain sight. It is the heart of the hearer that hides the mysteries of God from mankind, not their inability to be deciphered. Understanding the Kingdom is a capacity of the heart, not the mind. Therefore, that which affects the heart can alter our perceptions, how we hear, and ultimately our understanding of what we hear.

The parable of the sower and the seed illustrates the underlying conditions of the heart which corrupt our understanding by those who: 1) instantly reject the Word because of hardness of heart, 2) are shallow and because of persecution or pressures turn away, and 3) are deceived by the pleasures of this life and their desire for other things, sowing corrupt seed that is contradictory to God's Word, thereby choking it out. It is the condition of our hearts that determine whether the Word is understandable or incomprehensible to us. Confusion is a self-induced disordered mental state which arises from being presented with the truth but unwilling to repent. James 3:16 says, *"Where there is selfish ambition there is confusion..."* When we insist we do not understand, it is our religious justification for not believing the truth. Jesus explained how we close our eyes so we cannot see, our ears so we cannot hear and dull our hearts so we cannot understand (Matthew 13:15). Why? We never had any intention of surrendering our opinions in the first place; therefore, we refuse to repent.

When asked why Jesus taught in parables, a casual glance at the Scriptures would seem to indicate God was being selective toward whom He would and would not give revelation. But upon closer examination, we see that each of us makes our own choice whether or not we will hear and understand what God is saying. To such an absurd indictment against God's love of all men, Lenski says:

The Scripture answer: no unwillingness on God's part to give (1 Tim. 2:4; 2 Pet. 3:9; Jn. 3:16; Matt. 28:19-20) but only the unwillingness of so many to receive... (Matt. 23:37; Acts 7:51; Hos. 13:9)[1]

Our heavenly Father longs to reveal His mysteries of truth to everyone. He is

---

1   **P 511**, The Interpretation of St Matthew's Gospel, R.C.H. Lenski, Augsburg Publishing House, Minneapolis, MN, 1946

doing everything He can to draw all mankind to Jesus, other than violating our will. Love never violates the will of another person, even when that other person is being self-destructive. However, these things are only a mystery to those who will not hear. God has given us His written Word, and the Holy Spirit is persistently attempting to speak wisdom to our hearts. The more obvious revelation is the life and teachings of Jesus Himself; even when we cannot understand the complexities of who Jesus is, we can see how He lived.

Some form of the Gospel has been preached to most of the world. Scores of people who had never read the Bible or heard a sermon but deeply hungered to know the true God have reported receiving personal visitations from Jesus. In other words, people who want to know the truth will always find it. This leaves us with the ugly reality no one wants to admit: for many, ignorance and misunderstanding about God and His ways are largely preferable to repentance.

I am not saying that most people are going to *look God in the face* and say, *I reject your ways and choose mine*. I am saying that we find a false sense of security in doing things the way we have always done them, seeing things the way we have always seen them, and thinking the way we have always thought for so long that we will not trust any influence that does not support our predetermined perspective. Some studies indicate man's greatest fear is the fear of the unknown. Nowhere is this more apparent than when people stay in dysfunctional, often abusive relationships rather than risk the unknown. Sadly, people will continue in a destructive lifestyle rather than accept the offer of heaven on earth simply because they have never seen it.

The Amplified Bible gives a more accurate rendering of James 3:16 (AMPC), *"For wherever there is jealousy (envy) and contention (rivalry and selfish ambition), there will also be confusion (unrest, disharmony, rebellion) and all sorts of evil and vile practices."* Jealousy and selfishness are a continuum of lust, and *lust* is a desire. We believe that when that desire is fulfilled, it will bring great pleasure. *Jealousy* is often a component of the imagination that comes from coveting what someone else has, while *selfish ambition* is the commitment to have the things we so deeply desire; therefore, we hold fast to our secret agendas. Any thought, input, or suggestion from God or man about the destructiveness of our pursuit can be met with outright rejection or a stream of self-justification and rationalizations which leads to a state of self-induced confusion. When people know what to do but refuse to cease pursuing their lusts, the standard response is, "I am confused, or I do not understand." After 45 years of counseling, I discovered that "I do not understand," actually means "I do not want to understand."

To enter the kingdom, we must first see the door. The *door* is an entryway into being able to perceive that which is promised in the gospel. The first requirement is to perceive the door. Unrepentant hearts cannot be led or taught of the Lord; therefore, the Holy Spirit cannot lead them to the door. Not seeing the door is justification to the carnal mind that there is no door, and, thus, there is no ful-fillment for these promises, confirming that the carnal person's way makes more logical sense than something he cannot see.

God never asks you to make a commitment to something you cannot see or perceive. Contrary to religious logic, faith is never blind, and God cannot and will not violate your free will. Millions of people have discovered an incredible quality of life simply by sincerely praying, "I cannot see this, but if it is real, I am willing to see it. I am asking you to open my eyes, bring me to the place to see what I cannot see now."

HeartWork

Read This Aloud Before Every HeartWork Session: The Kingdom of God is internal. HeartWork is designed to remove any internal obstacles that prevent me from entering the realm where I experience Heaven on Earth!

1. Am I willing to allow God to show me something that may challenge many of my currently held beliefs?

2. Is there something I want but am afraid I will lose it if I follow God?

3. Have I sincerely prayed the prayer mentioned above?

CHAPTER 4

Recovering Sight

We only believe what we can see, and we can only see what we are willing to see!

Jesus miraculously gave sight to the physically blind, but not every scripture mentioning blind eyes being open is about the physically blind. In Luke 4, when Jesus launched His public ministry, He addressed the core reason our lives are in shambles: we have a broken heart. A ***broken or bruised heart*** is one that has been trampled on and is filled with pain so devastating it makes it impossible for us to live the abundant life.

One of the ways Jesus brings recovery is by opening the eyes of the ***blind.*** In this particular scripture, He is not referring to the physically blind but rather those who have been so hurt by life they cannot see the freedom God is offering. The prophet Isaiah spoke of those who sit in the darkness of a prison (Isa. 42:7-9, NIV). Jesus has opened the door to the prison, but the darkness that captivates the prisoner prevents the way out from being seen. The promise of a new life does not make sense to the person who perceives themselves as a prisoner who cannot escape. What we need is the eyes of our heart opened to perceive God's reality.

In Luke 4:18, the phrase Jesus used when He said He recovers *"sight to the blind"* is the same phrase used in Mark 6:41. With His natural eyes, Jesus saw the need: feeding 5,000 people with five loaves of bread and two fish. Because Jesus was tempted in every way just as we are[1], He had to recover His "spiritual sight." If

---

1   **Heb. 4:15**, "For we do not have a high priest who is unable to empathize with our weaknesses, but we have one who has been tempted in every way, just as we are-yet he did not sin." (NIV)

He had not seen the situation with the eyes of His heart, He would have been limited to His natural resources, which would have never met the need.

In verse 41 of Mark 6 it says, *"When He had taken the five loaves and the two fish, He looked up to heaven, blessed and broke the loaves...."* In the original language, this phrase actually says, *"He looked into heaven and recovered His sight."*[1] The word for **recovering sight** is the same as is used in Luke 4:18. Our heart is the seat of our insight, perception, understanding, and faith. A broken heart twists our perception, and our blindness is the darkness that makes truth unclear.

Although our broken heart may be imprisoned by darkness and we cannot see, our freedom of choice is always intact. At any time, we can open our hearts to God and recover our sight to see and perceive, to hear and understand. The moment we make a choice to simply be open to God, He is free to work in our lives. Only then can we perceive the Kingdom of God. For the person who has suffered from a broken heart, this message offers a promise too good to be true. How could someone who has been crushed by life ever allow themselves to hope for something so incredible? It's not impossible, but it is a mystery!

Jesus came declaring the mystery that the sages diligently sought to know its content and the timing of its appearance. The message most dreaded and feared by governments, kings, and those who lusted for power, including the devil himself was the revelation for which the meek, humble, and godly hunger and thirst: the Mystery of the Kingdom! To one group they were words of life, but to the other, they were the words of death. For the fearful and unbelieving who would not open their hearts, they were simply imperceptible.

In the Bible, we often see what appears to be contradictory concepts. One example is in the case of God hardening someone's heart. Tragically, this particular concept has been interpreted as God sovereignly choosing to harden some hearts while choosing to soften others. The problem with that interpretation is that it directly opposes aspects of God's loving nature. When Scripture appears to contradict itself, it is either a poor translation or a misunderstanding in our interpretation. Whether our hearts are hardened or softened by the truth we hear is determined by the condition of our hearts. Our immunity to lies and our affinity for truth is always determined by the condition of our hearts.

My first mentor helped me understand God's effect on Pharaoh's heart with this expression, "The same sun that softens butter hardens clay." The children of Israel rejoiced when God called them out to the wilderness to worship, but Pharaoh became enraged. The light of God's Word as it poured from the mouth of Jesus or as it is read from the pages of the Bible, is like the heat of the sun.

1   **(an-ab-lep'-o)**; from NT:303 and NT:991; to look up; by implication, to recover sight; Biblesoft's New Exhaustive Strong's Numbers and Concordance with Expanded Greek-Hebrew Dictionary. Copyright © 1994, 2003, 2006 Biblesoft, Inc. and International Bible Translators, Inc.

The question is whether your heart is like butter that becomes soft, pliable and yielding or like clay that becomes hard, inflexible and resistant.

Jesus told His disciples, "... *Unto you it is given to know the mysteries of the kingdom of God* .... " (Luke 8:10, KJV) Earlier, they were given a key that made it possible for them to understand His parables, even so, from time to time He had to explain them in greater detail. Even with more explanation, those who did not have this key would never understand.

A mystery is revealed through a process that begins with an initiation and is then revealed in stages or degrees. We all have a one-time event that begins a lifetime process of receiving the Kingdom of God. The million dollar question is: what is the one-time event that has such a dramatic effect on our heart that it changes our capacity to hear and understand God's Word of the Kingdom? (Matt. 13:19, NIV). The answer lies in the attitudes of the hearers.

The two main types of hearers who listened to the teachings of Jesus were believers and non-believers. Within the group of believers, there were two subcategories: those who were not disciples and those who were. A *disciple* is one who seeks to build and govern life by the teaching and lifestyle of the teacher. Prior to the resurrection, no one was born again, so it is not simply the new birth that opens our heart and mind to the capacity to understand.

A disciple that molds his or her life after the teaching and example of the teacher must have one trait above all others, a trait that goes beyond casual believing. After all, the demons believe and tremble (James 2:19, KJV), but they are certainly not disciples—they are enemies. A disciple believes and is teachable; predetermined to surrender or reject any opinion, doctrine or lifestyle contrary to the Master's teaching and example.

The disciple begins a journey with one predominant attitude: repentance! Contrary to the religious notion of repentance, the original language teaches that it is a continuing state of mind. We cannot be disciples of Jesus if we are unwilling to continuously surrender our thoughts, opinions, doctrines, and lifestyles to His teaching and example. The moment we, as believers, refuse to repent, we are no longer disciples. The Kingdom message John the Baptist prepared the people to hear was, *"Repent ye: for the kingdom of heaven is at hand!"* (Matt. 3:2, ESV). This was the explicit and implicit message in all of Jesus's teaching, and as such, repentance is the one preparatory decision for becoming a disciple, for it is this attitude and decision that opens our hearts to receive what God is offering to all men: the capacity, or the *grace*, to understand.

Repentance is not the door to the Kingdom, but it does reveal the door. Those who are not ready to surrender themselves to the Lordship of Jesus, through repentance, are not even aware there is a door. The door of the Kingdom, which is the heart, can only be perceived when we are ready to surrender ourselves to

Jesus as Lord and become a disciple.

The Hebrew word for hear and obey is the same word. Hearing and obeying follow along a continuum, which helps us to better understand the concept: "The same sun that melts butter hardens clay." God, in His love, is calling out to all but not all are willing to hear. The heart can only hear, see and perceive that which it is willing to do. The repentant heart is truly ready and willing to follow anything God says, and can, therefore, hear, see, perceive and understand.

We all want God to open our eyes so we can know how to make decisions and navigate life, but the reality is that God cannot open our eyes when we have chosen to keep them closed. To do so would violate our will, and that is one thing God can never and will never do.

Heart Work

Read This Aloud Before Every HeartWork Session: The Kingdom of God is internal. HeartWork is designed to remove any internal obstacles that prevent me from entering the realm where I experience Heaven on Earth!

Before moving on, it is essential to make a clear and honest evaluation of your relationship with Jesus. I am not asking you to question your salvation, but it is important to decide if you will approach Him as a disciple and relate to Him as your Lord.

1.   Have I made an absolute commitment to follow the teachings and lifestyle of Jesus?

2.   Do I surrender my every doctrine, tradition, opinion, and behavior to His teaching and example?

3.   If not, am I ready to do so now?

4.   I understand that if I want my eyes open to see God's perfect plan for my life, I must open them.

CHAPTER 5

Trusting Your Opinion or Trusting God

Every man lives by faith, but not necessarily faith in God!

Faith is an issue of the heart. The word **faith**, in a very general sense, identifies what or whom we trust. Our every decision is made based on what we believe and trust. Since faith is a function of the heart, whether it is faith in God or faith in our personal feelings and opinions, it has the power to make what we believe come to pass. People often believe they will die at a certain age and they do. People believe they will get cancer and they do. People believe they will overcome problems and they do. The testimonials that prove faith can work for or against us are endless. The truth is we all live by faith; it is just rarely faith in God and the wisdom of His counsel. From this point forward when speaking of faith, I will be addressing faith in God unless otherwise stated.

Our every struggle, offense, and temptation is the fruit of what we think and believe. Thoughts give rise to emotions, and beliefs create deep-seated feelings.[1] Our feelings and emotions drive our behavior, thereby projecting our inner struggles onto the world around us, multiplying the problem and magnifying the scope of conflict or cure to all with whom we interact. When our inner struggles become social, we tend to focus on external behavior for solutions instead of internal beliefs.

Since beliefs are the subconscious driving force behind our behavior, problems are only permanently resolved when our beliefs are changed; otherwise, we live in a suspended state of feelings versus willpower. Many Christians face this tor-

1   *Moving Your Invisible Boundaries: the Key to Limitless Living*, Dr. Jim Richards, 2013, True Potential, Inc., SC www.truepotentialmedia.com

menting struggle because the modern church totally ignores the integral role and function of our hearts. How ironic that the heart, the core of every aspect of our connection with God, is totally disregarded beyond a few token references.

Changing beliefs lead to an effortless change in thinking, feeling,[1] emotions, and ultimately behavior. While behavior modification is not wrong, it is only temporary; it will last only as long as our willpower is present. But, because behavior modification reduces social conflict, it is often seen as a victory. Behavior modification can, however, be an effective tool when the reprieve from social angst is used to resolve the real problem: the beliefs of our hearts.

Religion is a system of relating to God on man's terms instead of God's terms. Religion uses biblical terminology but changes the definitions. It is a very subtle form of propaganda designed to rob the believer of true biblical faith. Religion, while looking and sounding spiritual, is based on unbelief in what God says about Himself. It alters what we see, perceive and believe about God, thereby altering what we can trust about Him. It also alters how we interpret God's Word. Religion is a combination of external performance, mysticism, and humanism, all of which are rooted in *Luciferianism*.

Faith is man's response of trust to God, based on His testimony of Himself. Faith trusts what God says because it trusts who God is. Religion is man's attempt to evoke a response from God based on a formula, ritual or personal performance and is rooted in man's opinion of God. Man's opinion is a vain imagination, and it is this imagination wherein man creates false religions, idols and faulty concepts of God. Instead of carving an image from wood or stone we engrave a false image in our mind and heart. Our response to one of God's most important questions: "Who has believed our report?"[2] is always a response of either faith or religion.

Religion is a deceptive, toxic and deadly mixture of truth and lies. As one of my favorite preachers used to say, "Religion is like a vaccine; it gives you just enough of the real thing that you cannot catch it!" The most deadly aspect, however, is that religion appeals to the logic of the carnal mind. As previously mentioned, religion uses biblical words and terminology, but it alters their definitions. As casual listeners who will not read the Bible to understand for ourselves nor allow the Holy Spirit to be our Teacher, we think we are hearing the Word of God, when in fact, we are only learning the words in the Bible. In reality, we are learning the doctrine of demons! Our doctrines shape the beliefs of our heart - the seat of our love, faith, wisdom, and understanding.

Religion preaches *propaganda* designed to shape our worldview and personal perception by determining how we perceive God. The *propaganda gospel* is

1   *Moving Your Invisible Boundaries: the Key to Limitless Living*, Dr. Jim Richards, 2013, True Potential, Inc., SC www.truepotentialmedia.com
2   **Isa. 53:1**, "Who hath believed our report? And to whom is the arm of the Lord revealed?" (KJV) 1 Peter 1:12

designed to give authority to institutions and/or to those "anointed to lead." Rather than leading the believer into a personal relationship with God where the individual is submitted to the Lordship of Jesus, it brings the worshipper into submission to a person, **denomination**, group or doctrine. The irony is that this life-destroying deception is reinforced with Christian terminology, such as "The Lord Jesus Christ or surrender to the will of God," but the application reveals its true definition. Surrender and submission are not to God but to a vain imagination resulting in a constant dependency on those who pretend to have the power to reveal God to you!

Since these definitions and concepts are learned while we are in pursuit of God or our idea of God - and they come from people with position, recognition, respect, and authority - we, as mere laymen, cannot challenge nor dissent. *Laymen* or *laity* means "common or ordinary." Some have said it literally means: "the nothing ones." This distinction between laity, or the nothing ones, and *clergy*, i.e. "the anointed ones," creates a class distinction which includes the right to study and understand Scripture personally. By distinction, those teaching us have the anointing to understand Scripture, and therefore, must serve as mediators between us and God to ensure that as ignorant laymen we do not find ourselves opposing denominational doctrine. Their interpretation of Scripture becomes laws by which we must live, thereby corrupting our understanding so we can never quite see God as He is or understand the Word of the Kingdom (Matt. 13:19, NIV) for ourselves. We can neither see the door or enter the door!

Jesus warned that tradition or culture could actually neutralize the Word of God, rendering it ineffective in our lives. The tradition against which He spoke was the teaching of the Jews which interpreted the Word of God, thereby dictating its application. Once this happens, we are seldom, if ever, following God or even the Word of God; we are following the traditional interpretation of the Word and the dictates of religious propaganda. Thus, while speaking the name of God and quoting His Word, we are etching our beliefs about God on to our heart, believing and obeying someone else's interpretation of God's Word, rendering the actual Word of God ineffective. The harder we attempt to grow in our faith the less faith in God we actually have. *I know mine do you know yours?*

The Jews means of propaganda was the priesthood and the law. In this, our ignorance of Jewish history limits our understanding of the <u>term **law**</u>. Every place in the New Testament where the law is spoken of in a negative way, it is not talking about the commandments God spoke; it is talking about the Jewish laws that interpreted God's commandments. Every word of Jesus and every teaching of the Apostles were based on the <u>commandments</u>. God's Word is not, nor has it ever been, legalistic or fear-based, but man's religious interpretation and application have been absolutely fear-based and legalistic.

With their lips, the Jews venerated the name and Word of God, but as Jesus

Because of the law (some 613) not the ONLY 10

pointed out, their hearts are far from Him! Over the centuries, the Jews compiled many books written by the sages in what they called the Talmud, in which they attempted to interpret how to apply Scripture. The Talmud can have many benefits in understanding Jewish history and even some word translation. The Jewish leaders, however, violated the heart to heart relationship between God and man: instead of teaching people to learn the Word of God and apply it to their lives as the Holy Spirit led, the religious leaders interpreted how the Word of God should be applied, totally violating man's personal connection with God. The result was that the Talmud became the basis for all teaching rather than Scripture, a rendering that was twisted in its meaning: propaganda!

Like the Jews of Jesus's day, we have grown up under the indoctrination of not just religious leaders, but parents, teachers and political figures who have defined every aspect of life and how it should be lived. Their ideology has become the foundation of our belief system. One of the famous rules of propaganda is this: a person will believe the lie they hear repeatedly. In a wartime report written by psychoanalyst Walter C. Langer, which was later published in a book entitled, *The Mind of Adolf Hitler,* he writes, "People will believe a big lie sooner than a little one, and if you repeat it frequently enough, people will sooner or later believe it." What we have heard about love, marriage, sex, morality, politics, God, faith, health, money, and every other conceivable aspect of life was not taught to us by God and His Word, but by those who, perhaps with good intentions, have sought to shape our views to match theirs.

Some professionals say our every thought is based on a memory or an imagination. Sadly, most of our imagination is limited to the confines of our memories. Suffice it to say, most of our creativity is based on what we have already been told, which limits our capacity to see the world beyond the influence of our tradition. What few of us are willing or capable of admitting is that before coming to Jesus we may have never had an original thought, and since coming to Jesus, until we **renew our minds**, what seems to be revelation or new insight may actually be a revision of something we learned in the past. When we trust God more than we trust ourselves, we realize how easy and beneficial it is to admit they we may not have a single opinion about any aspect of our life that is actually in harmony with the Word of God.

Joseph Goebbels, Hitler's Propaganda Minister, said, "The best propaganda is that which, as it were, works invisibly, penetrates the whole of life without the public having any knowledge of the propagandistic initiative." I would take it a step further and say, "The most influential propaganda is spread by those with good intentions who have no consciousness they are actually spreading propaganda." The passion of sincerity has spread more propaganda than any other proponent of society. Unless we surrender our every thought and opinion to the Word of God as interpreted by the life, teaching, application, death, burial, and resurrection of Jesus, there is a high probability that much of our sharing, preaching and life application is actually recycled propaganda.

We spend our lives being brainwashed, much of which has occurred through the annals of religion or the propaganda of false science or government. Having been influenced by religion, we have multiple ways in which to proliferate the effects of our lifetime of propaganda. We will focus on two of those possibilities: reject God's Word altogether or humble ourselves to God and allow the Holy Spirit to teach us. Most people I have counseled over the past 40 years came to Jesus with great intentions; however, never having renewed their minds, their beliefs, opinions and general life paradigm never changed. They embedded their own opinions into biblical definitions of words and engaged in *Christian-ese* without actually repenting from their established worldview. While speaking God's name and using biblical terminology, they employed a faith made of their own opinion without ever really seeking to know God's.

Subsequently, after years of attempting to make religious propaganda accomplish what the professionals said it should accomplish, they finally realized they had been seduced by religion. Then, in what appears to be a bold launch into true spiritual freedom, they rejected as much doctrine as they could. Instead of using biblical tools to read and study the Word with the intention of following the Holy Spirit as their Teacher, they simply rejected religious propaganda, succeeding only to reject God altogether. They failed to realize they only needed to reject the false definitions and concepts of God that religion has defined for us, not God's Word. So rather than rejecting the false definition of church, they rejected the church; instead of rejecting the false definition of faith, they rejected faith; by despising the false definition of repentance, they rejected repentance. While proclaiming themselves free, they were taken captive by a deception far worse than anything to which they had been seduced: rejection of God's Word. Instead of truth guarding their heart, through fear and anger, they guard their heart by hardening it and once again rendering themselves incapable of ever seeing the door to the Kingdom.

The only process for **transformation** in the New Covenant involves putting off the old man, renewing the mind and putting on the new man. All of this demands that we address our thoughts and beliefs, all of which are ultimately expressed in our behavior. This entire process is rooted in repentance, not just a one-time repentance but a dynamic harmonization between the mind and heart that continuously fine-tunes our mindset. Repentance is the starting place for surrender to Jesus as Lord and a lifetime of discipleship. We cannot learn anything new if our heart and mind will not surrender its view and opinion to God. We cannot simultaneously hold on to what we have and take hold of something new. We cannot travel north as long as we continue to travel south. And we cannot see what God is attempting to show us as long as we insist we already see!

Renewing the mind, through a very specific biblical process, is the only way we can see where our thoughts and beliefs are in disharmony with God and, more importantly, see how to bring the Word into our lives in a way that is relevant and life-giving. Renewing the mind is the fulcrum for putting off the old man and putting on the new man. Renewing the mind is not a mere intellectual process; it is coming to know Jesus as Lord, the Holy Spirit as Teacher, God as our gentle, wise Father and His Word as the one tool for directing our lives to the fullest potential. Renewing the mind is a process that begins with the choice to trust God's view and opinion more than our own. In the most simple terms: it is when we realize God is smarter than we are!

Like all Kingdoms, the King's Word is the truth. The convert is not seeking to earn entrance into the Kingdom; they are seeking to renew their mind, so they know how to function in the Kingdom. This process of renewing the mind is only possible to those with a repentance attitude and a teachable mind! One of our greatest challenges is to have more faith in God than our personal opinions.

HeartWork

Read This Aloud Before Every HeartWork Session: The Kingdom of God is internal. HeartWork is designed to remove any internal obstacles that prevent me from entering the realm where I experience Heaven on Earth!

1. Where did I get my beliefs about God and every aspect of life?

2. Do I personally and diligently study to ensure my beliefs align with God's Word?

3. Do I allow others to influence my view of life and God? If so, who?

4. Do they validate their opinion with the Word of God?

CHAPTER 6

Everything Starts with Faith In God

You cannot have faith for what God will do apart from faith for who He is!

When we come to Jesus, whether we realize it or not, we are searching for the Kingdom, which takes us to a quality of life better than anything we have ever experienced. After all, most people come to Jesus when they realize their approach to life is not working—they want a better life. The general hope given to people in their great need is: "Jesus is the answer." That may or nor may not be a true statement. What we believe in our heart when we say "Jesus is the answer" determines if we are telling the truth, and how the hearer interprets it is determined by whether or not they believe the truth.

Sadly, modern converts tend to think that believing on Jesus to save them is sufficient to solve all their problems. After all, they were told Jesus is the answer. Real life experience proves that is never the case. Herein lies a paradox that few seem to grasp. Salvation is not a one-dimensional event. It is the experiential first step of a lifetime journey. On earth, that journey is consummated in the heart of the believer who enters the realm of the Kingdom.

The only way to understand the New Covenant life of a believer is to understand the Old Testament journey of the children of Israel from Egypt to Canaan. All their struggles are types of the struggles we face today. Like Israel, we just do not trust God to deliver some of His promises. So often the circumstances are greater than our capacity to trust God. The Apostle Paul reminds us in 1 Corinthians 10:1-11, everything that happened to the children of Israel are examples for us. We can see where and why they stumbled, but we can also see when and why they prevailed. All these events were recorded in God's Word for us: those who live under the New Covenant and are seeking to enter into the Kingdom of God.

The writer of Hebrews lays out a very clear parallel between the journey of the Israelites and the journey of the New Covenant believer. He presents the compelling typology of Canaan as an example of entering into rest, which seems to be synonymous with the Kingdom of God. By understanding their struggles, we can trust God's word rather than learning by trial and error; we can learn by their example, forego the pain of failure and move into this place of rest known as the Kingdom of God.

To properly interpret Scripture, we must first understand what Scripture is. Every word of the New Testament is based on Scripture–the Old Testament. Jesus, all of the Apostles and the early church called it the Scripture. The writers of the New Testament never considered their writings to be a replacement of Scripture. They were not a replacement; they were an interpretation and instruction about application based on the New Covenant.

Pagan influence began to enter the church through the Gentile converts who did not know the Scripture. Instead of interpreting and applying the writings of the Apostles based on Scripture, they interpreted them from pagan philosophies like Gnosticism and asceticism. Classifying the Bible into Old and New Testaments created a false separation between the history of God as revealed in Scripture and the life, teaching, and resurrection of Jesus. This separation was essential. If the Scriptures were the body of knowledge about God, Catholicism would have clearly been condemned as an idolatrous, pagan religion; therefore, there was a need to corrupt the faith by separating them from the scriptures.

It is impossible to actually understand most of what Jesus taught without a working knowledge of the Old Testament. Likewise, the Old Testament cannot be properly interpreted apart from the New Testament. Neither can stand independently! The rejection of the Old Testament opened the door for occult and pagan doctrines to fill the early church. Most Luciferian doctrine came into the church through the Gentile believers who were utterly ignorant of the Old Testament. It was, on the other hand, primarily the Jewish converts who, without the New Testament, flooded the early church with legalism; therefore, faith was based more on the doctrine of the church than in the knowledge of God.

Upon closer examination of both the New Testament and Old Testament Scripture, we can understand what it means to enter into the Kingdom of God. Through concise overviews of several meaningful events, I am attempting only to provide clarity for the modern day believer; however, there are greater depths of understanding in the typology of all of Paul's writings:

Egypt is a type of the world. As slaves, the Israelites had no choice but to obey their masters. Being slaves to sin, we have no choice but to obey our lusts. I encourage you to study the Exodus account for yourself and discover the wealth of insight that can be gained.

- The children of Israel left Egypt on the night of the first Passover. The 10 plagues were poured out on Egypt as a way to break the hold of the Egyptians and provide deliverance for Israel. The one provision that protected the Israelites from the fate of Egypt (the world) was the blood of the lamb.

- Before partaking in the Passover Lamb, they observed what became the feast of unleavened bread. *Leaven* is usually seen as sin, but, more than anything, leaven is a way of thinking. While all sin has the power to destroy, it is the leaven - the unrenewed mind - that is the actual culprit. What did they have to change that had so much potential to derail all that God was doing for them? They had to surrender everything they had learned for how to live while under the pagan influence of the Egyptians (the world). More importantly, they had to surrender every concept of God as the world's system defined Him.

- Early in their exodus from Egypt, we see the parable of the sower and the seed being expressed. Just like this Kingdom parable explains, there are many ways we allow the seed of God's Word to be robbed from us. In this particular instance, the Israelites never allowed the Word to be rooted in their hearts. Upon reaching "the land of milk and honey"–a type of the Kingdom of God–they could not enter in to experience the life God promised, just like so many people who become "Christians" but never make the journey of faith from Egypt into the Kingdom realm.

- Crossing the Red Sea was a type of being baptized into the body of Christ.

- Receiving the Law at Mount Sinai was a type of the Word of God being written on our hearts.

- Crossing the Jordan River was very probably a type of the baptism in the Holy Spirit, wherein we receive the power (grace and wisdom) to conquer our enemies, i.e., our flesh which wars against our soul.

- Driving out the nations that inhabited the land represents the different characteristics of our flesh.

- What should have been approximately an eleven-day journey through the wilderness turned into 40 years before they entered the Promised Land. Why didn't God simply make it happen supernaturally? The wilderness journey is a type of the carnal mind, which embodies many subtleties of destructive thinking and actions. The theme of the book of Leviticus is "be holy as I am holy." When something is **holy,** it is uncommon. God taught them all the ways that He was completely unlike all the pagan gods. One way, in particular, was that sacrifices were not designed to appease His wrath; they were always intended as a means for operating faith to influence their hearts and reconnect with God. Offerings were never given to draw God near to them, but rather an act of faith in drawing near to Him. He was a God of love and relationship, ever reaching out to His people. They were to see themselves as sons and citizens of a holy nation, in preparation to be the light of God's love shining in a dark world.

All of the promises God made were contingent on two factors: seeing God as He is and seeing themselves as God saw them. Remember, they were slaves, not only of the Egyptian people but of the Egyptians gods. For hundreds of years, they were surrounded by paganism while having it forced upon them. Pharaoh himself was considered to be a god; therefore, to serve Pharaoh was to serve another god.

Naturally, they viewed themselves as slaves and the gods as their brutal masters, and, as such, slaves do not want a relationship with their masters. All slaves want to know is what they must do to keep their masters satisfied and how to avoid their wrath. The Israelites' unbelief in the wilderness was merely a projection of their faulty view of God and of themselves. Trusting in a god who had made promises to his slaves was completely foreign to them.

The Bible explicitly explains why the children of Israel could not enter into the Promised Land because of their unbelief[1]: the Word they heard did not benefit them because they did not mix it with faith[2]. Nearly the entire fouth chapter of Hebrews warns us not to suffer that same fate. It is clearly saying that, even though we are born-again believers, it does not automatically mean we will enter into this place of God's rest, i.e., the Kingdom of God.

This next concept is probably one of the most difficult to grasp. We all agree with the premise but seldom comprehend what it may look like in real life application. God is more interested in who we are than what we do, or it could be said that God is more interested in us *being* than *doing*; nevertheless, *being* and *doing* are a continuum. The seed is the *being*, while the fruit is the *doing*. Since *being* is a heart issue, the only way we can validate that we are who we say we are is by the fruit we produce. If what we do is contradictory with Godly character, it proves that we are not yet who we say we are.

God taught the children of Israel who He was and they were called to be like

---

1   **Heb. 3:19**, "So we see that they could not enter in because of unbelief." (KJV)
2   **Heb. 4:2**, "For unto us was the gospel preached, as well as unto them: but the word preached did not profit them, not being mixed with faith in them that heard it."

Him: generous, kind, merciful, honest, moral and ethical–in all ways Godly. Even if He drove out all the inhabitants of Canaan and they walked in to claim the land uninhibited, they still could not have been the people they needed to be to possess it. Unbelief renders us incapable of being the people who can live in the promises of God!

Picture the scenario of a man who is believing for a beautiful, loving wife. Now imagine that God brings the woman of his dreams into his life. He talks a good game, expresses all the right values, and she is immediately attracted to him. They have a whirlwind romance and get married. On the outside, it appears that the promise has been fulfilled.

Not long after their marriage, however, she begins to realize he is not the man she thought he was. He had good intentions and continued to say all the right words, but at every turn he manages himself in a way that disproves his assumed identity. In response to her growing discontent, he desperately cries out to God to save their marriage, but the truth is that he is the only one who can save his marriage by being the man who can live with such an incredible woman. As I have told men for decades: if you want to marry Mrs. Right and have a great marriage, all you have to do is be Mr. Right!

God was calling the children of Israel to trust and follow Him, but not just to the Promised Land. He needed them to be the people who would trust Him as He led them through every battle of life, every challenge and every disaster, all the way to victory.

The length of time it takes us to get from Egypt to Canaan is up to us–not God. He has already done His part to create the promises and the path that leads to them. The question is whether or not we believe He is who He says He is, we are who He says we are, and if we desire to actually be the righteousness of God: those who can enter into the Promised Land and possess the promises?

Every aspect of faith begins with believing that God is who He has declared Himself to be. Faith in God is not merely believing He exists; it is believing He is the rewarder of those who diligently seek Him, that He is who His names declare Him to be, and most importantly, that He is exactly as Jesus represented Him. We can only believe God can and will keep His promises to the degree we believe He is who He claims to be, and we can only become like Him when we see Him as He really is.

The Gospel of the Kingdom is unbelievable on every level until we believe the truth about God. The wilderness journey from Egypt to possessing Canaan (the Kingdom) forces us to face all of our leaven: the beliefs we have formed from this world's system. Upon facing them, we will either choose to continue in the way of the world or go the way of God. And if we choose to go God's way, we must be willing to face all the nations–traits of the flesh–that we must allow to die so

God can give us the victories over all the issues that rob us from experiencing His quality of life. We will only do that if we choose to believe Him about His identity, our own identity and intend to be like Him as He really is!

HeartWork

Read This Aloud Before Every HeartWork Session: The Kingdom of God is internal. HeartWork is designed to remove any internal obstacles that prevent me from entering the realm where I experience Heaven on Earth!

1. Do I know the names of God?

2. Do I interpret scripture in harmony with the meanings of those names? An excellent resource for studying the names of God is The Prayer Organizer: https://www.impactministries.com/product/the-prayer-organizer/

3. Do I see that Jesus perfectly represented the identity of God?

4. Do I believe that if I desire and commit myself to it, God will transform me to be like Jesus?

CHAPTER 7

Too Good To Be True

When something is too good to be true, it usually is not true, unless God says it is

The word **gospel**, like so many biblical words, has taken on a colloquial meaning that is unrelated to what it actually means in Scripture. When swearing that something is true, many people will declare, "It is gospel!" In most religious settings the word *gospel* represents a specific idea vaguely related to Jesus and salvation, but people with some biblical knowledge agree that the most accepted definition of gospel is "good news."

While *gospel* can mean "good news," it can also mean "the reward for good news." The Theological Dictionary of the New Testament says:

The spoken word is equated with its content; bad news brings sorrow and good news joy. The bearer of bad news is thus guilty and may be punished for it, while the bearer of good news is rewarded.[1]

Interestingly, this concept brings a new dimension to determining what is and what is not gospel. The obvious questions we should ask to determine if a statement is gospel are: 1) is this in the scriptural fulfillment of Jesus's resurrection, and 2) does it produce joy or sorrow for the hearer? Jesus brought good news that: brings joy about the Kingdom of God, is available to all, can be entered into by anyone at any time, is not hard like the religious leaders portrayed it and makes it possible to connect directly to God without going through the religious hierarchy.

1   ***Theological Dictionary of the New Testament***, abridged edition, Copyright © 1985 by William B. Eerdmans Publishing Company.

When Jesus preached salvation, it was apparent to the listener that He was talking about a quality of life here on earth. Paul described it this way, *"Eye hath not seen, nor ear heard, neither have entered into the heart of man, the things which God has prepared for them who love Him. But God hath revealed them unto us through His Spirit...."* (1 Cor. 2:9-10, KJV) The Gospel is something so good, it is beyond the experience or imagination. It is so good, it can only be revealed by the Holy Spirit.

Because of our Gentile misconceptions about salvation we tend to miss this mystery called the *Kingdom of God.* Salvation, the Kingdom of God and the Kingdom of Heaven came to mean that which is experienced only after we die. The original language, however, clearly refers to an experience that occurs in this life and continues into eternity. Another reason this is such good news is that it could be experienced independently of the actions or will of others. Religion, in an attempt to control the believer, has emphasized suffering as a prerequisite for the inheritance in the after-life. Fortunately, this Luciferian doctrine is neither in the Old or New Testaments.

According to many Hebrew teachers, when a Jew heard Jesus speak of the Kingdom of God, they probably thought of Eden. In fact, the Garden of Eden represents both the Kingdom of God and the Kingdom of Heaven. From this, we understand that the Kingdom of God is a place where its inhabitants are surrendered to the King. Eden represents one of the clearest ways to understand God's will for man. It was the environment God chose for man, not based on anyone's prayers or any human's faith. Dispensationalists[1] would argue that, since man became sin, God's will for them changed, but this contradicts the fact that He is the great "I Am" who never changes. The theological concept of Dispensationalism used to explain away what we do not understand is predicated only by that which our carnal mind will not believe.

As long as man trusted and yielded to God, they lived in His perfect will where there was no sin, sickness or lack of any kind! The curse that came on the earth was not God's punishment for sin; it was the consequences of man's choices. As man dominated planet earth, it evolved into what he desired...a world ruled by men without God's wisdom, hence the scripture that says, *"... Cursed is the ground because of you."* (Gen. 3:17, NASB) It does not say God cursed the earth. The King James Version clearly states that the earth was cursed for "your sakes." The root word for "your sakes" points to that which changed because of what was in their hearts.

Eden was also a place of incredible provision, producing everything man needed in the perfect form in which he needed it. The Garden, a type of the heart, was created with perfect soil, in a perfect environment and ripe with perfect seeds.

---

1   Dispensationalism is a religious interpretive system for the Bible. It considers biblical history as divided by God into periods or ages to which God reveals Himself and His truth to mankind.

It was understood, when referring to the Kingdom of God, to be a place where God ruled, and the Kingdom of heaven was a place where one had access to all God's resources. Even still, as great as Eden was, the gospel of the Kingdom promised something even better.

The cornerstone of faith, remember, is rooted in trusting God and starts with what we believe about creation. The person who does not believe the literal biblical account of creation will never have fully stable faith. If the foundation of all creation is treated as a myth, it is hard to trust God about anything refuted by secular science. While we cannot delve any further into this here, we now know that everything about the biblical account of creation has been mathematically proven, as is referenced in my book *Apocalypse*.[1]

The reason it was easy for the ordinary Jew to believe in Jesus's promise of the Kingdom is that they knew it had once existed. The very concept of Eden also made it easy to understand the need to surrender to Lordship. The Jewish mindset fully understood from Scripture that access to God's resources was the byproduct of being intimately connected to Him as Father, protector, provider, etc.

Although it was an imperfect type of the Kingdom, Eden was the best reference the Jews had for understanding God's intention toward them. They, of course, had no way to know that their nation and its history was the type for the New Covenant believer. The Apostles, however, clearly saw the history of Israel coming out of Egypt, every step of the wilderness journey, what befell them and ultimately possessing Canaan to be the perfect model for the life of a believer.

Canaan was an inheritance they would receive by a promise. God would lead them every step of the journey, but as we know He could only lead them where they would trust and follow. As Paul pointed out to the Corinthians, as well as by the writer of Hebrews, being a Christian is no guarantee for entering into the Kingdom—the place of rest. We must trust Him to obey Him, for only the obedient will truly follow Him into Kingdom living.

God led the Israelites to the Jordan River where He was ready and willing to deliver the nation of Canaan and its inhabitants into their hand. Due to their unbelief (rooted in how they saw God and themselves), they would not follow Him into Canaan. God had no choice but to keep them in the desert until a new generation arose that was willing to trust Him.

The legalist looks at their 40 years of wandering and labels it God's wrath when the more prevalent idea is that this massive group of people considered Him to be a liar who could not deliver what He promised. If God's wrath was as religion defined it, He would have simply killed them. Instead, He guided and protected them from hostile nations who sought their destruction, waiting patiently until

1   *Apocalypse: A Spiritual Guide to the Second Coming*, Dr. Jim Richards, 2015, True Potential, Inc., SC www.truepotentialmedia.com

a generation arose that would actually trust His promise and follow Him into the inheritance.

It seems the majority of believers live in the wilderness, experiencing degrees of God's provision and protection, but never really entering into the realm Jesus identified as the Kingdom of God. Like the children of Israel, they never admit to their own unbelief. Religion is continuously shoving more programs and formulas at them promising the outcome they desire, but it always falls short. Little do they realize that God is delivering unto them as much as their hearts will receive!

Both Jesus and Paul insisted on the need to experience the Holy Spirit as Teacher, Comforter and the One who imbues us with the power to do what needs to be done to enter into all God promises. This brings us to one of the greatest paradoxes of the Kingdom of God: the Holy Spirit is the one who opens our eyes to perceive that which is better than anything we have seen, heard or imagined, while another great paradox exists, which can only be resolved by the Holy Spirit.

God promised to deliver the land of Canaan to the Israelites, but they still had to fight the battles. The same is true for the New Covenant believer: we fight the battle, but we do so dependent and trusting in God's power to be our strength. The Holy Spirit, according to the Greek, is "the one called alongside to help." He is not called alongside to do! Like the children of Israel, we fail to grasp this subtle difference. They were going into battle, with their lives on the line, against superior forces and trained armies. Having been slaves who had never been trained for war, trusting God as their source for their victory meant the difference between life or death.

Their doubt stemmed from a combination of not believing in themselves and not believing in God. For us, that problem is resolved first by the fact that we are new creations in Christ. Second, we too have been delivered out of Egypt–our old nature. Finally, we have all the Word of God as proven history and every reason to trust God to be faithful to what He has promised. When we believe God is who He presents Himself to be and that we are who He says we are in Jesus, nothing will keep us from our inheritance: the Kingdom of God.

Every promise for a life this great just seems too good to be true. It seems beyond the reach of our faith, but one thing of which we can be sure: if we choose to take God at His Word and open our hearts, He will teach and guide us to the Kingdom realm, a way of living better than anything we have ever hoped, dreamed or imagined.

HeartWork

Read This Aloud Before Every HeartWork Session: The Kingdom of God is internal. HeartWork is designed to remove any internal obstacles that prevent me from entering the realm where I experience Heaven on Earth!

1. Have I chosen to believe God in every situation, even when I realize I am not confident enough to take steps of faith at this moment?

2. Do I choose to believe in the realm called the Kingdom of God even though I may not fully understand it?

3. Can I admit my limiting beliefs without guilt and shame?

4. Am I actually willing to believe and follow God in this pursuit?

CHAPTER 8

The Mystery of the Kingdom

The most difficult mystery to solve is the one hidden in plain sight!

The Kingdom of God is a mystery. As such, it can never be grasped by intellectual prowess alone. Based on the original language, this mystery can never be unraveled in any way other than making the journey into the Kingdom, which is a lifetime journey. Any time we stop making the journey, we stop grasping and growing in the mystery. As such, entering into the mystery of the Kingdom can never happen simply by being taught. Our inheritance of the Kingdom is very personal, occurring just between us and Jesus as Lord.

All things related to God are matters of the heart. The intellect plays a role, but it is a minimal role. The mind has to be renewed by the Word of God, but only the Holy Spirit, working in the heart, can bring wisdom and understanding. It is in the heart that information has the potential to become life. The paradox of this great mystery is this: children can understand what the wise of this world cannot because of the way they approach it. It is easily seen by those who have no agendas or predetermined dogma. The heart that fully trusts and is ready to repent at the first indication of incongruence between personal opinion and God's Word, easily grasps the many nuances of the Kingdom of God.

The word mystery in the Greek refers to something hidden or secret; it is discovered by initiation and is then revealed by degrees through the process of assimilation and then furthered by repeating that process in different areas. Assimilation is not the mere gathering and memorizing of intellectual information; it is the appropriation of God's revealed knowledge, wherewith we renew our mind.

We then write this information on the tables our heart by thinking, pondering, reflecting and meditating until it becomes our reality. Then, after we have established it as a belief of our heart, it manifests as a life-giving experience with transformative power. In this mystery, if you cannot get it to work in your life, you do not actually understand the mystery.

Luciferian cults have used these initiations since man partook of the tree of the knowledge of good and evil. The offer of a mystery that promises a way to have all God has promised through secret knowledge has been the seduction of millions. Offering people a way to have what God promises, but without God and His "pesky commandments" can be very seductive for the person not committed to godliness; however, they never reveal the depths of their corrupt logic or even their true intention until a person has gone through many initiation rites and has become fully brainwashed at each stage of the process.

God's Kingdom, as we have seen, is also hidden, not because God makes it difficult to see but because the conditions of our hearts hide it from us. The pure in heart, i.e., the one with no hidden motive or selfish interests and is true in all things, can see God...as He is. God is clear and up-front about what He offers and what it will require of us; there are no secret agendas. Between God's pure heart and the pure heart of the believer, a heart to heart connection is established, paving the journey ahead with clarity, understandability and even some predictability. Our journey into the realm of the Kingdom starts with a repentant, teachable attitude that surrenders to Jesus as Lord, which is equivalent to a commitment to God's Word as Jesus taught it. We have every reason to believe that repentance is the first key that makes it possible for us to realize there is a door which leads to the mystery realm of the Kingdom.

The door to the Kingdom is in our heart; it is not an external Kingdom nor will it be until Jesus returns the second time to personally overthrow the antichrist and his armies and to establish a physical Kingdom here on planet earth. His eternal Kingdom will be established when all wickedness is removed from the renovated earth, and then, New Jerusalem will come to earth where we will live eternally as God originally intended.

Religion has reduced Jesus's teaching of the Kingdom to simply being born again. If, however, the parables of the Kingdom are about how to be born again and get to heaven, Jesus preached salvation by works, not faith and grace. By diminishing his teaching, the Kingdom is nothing more than an automated process that occurs when a person is saved, bringing monumental dimensions of confusion and frustration to the believer who is expecting heaven on earth completely independent of the freedom of choice and faith When the believer's life does not automatically improve, the alternatives are few:

1.   Doubt our salvation

2. Turn to legalism and dead works as a way to earn the Kingdom benefits

3. Interpret Jesus's teaching to be about performance and not the heart

4. Reject Jesus's teaching

5. Turn the gospel into mythical and religious dogma

6. Reject the gospel entirely as inoperative

7. Create personal concepts about Jesus, independent of God's Word

The Kingdom of God and of Heaven are mysteries that can never be perceived, believed, understood or entered into by the unrepentant, unteachable heart. Although the promises of God should be a source of comfort, hope, and strength, they will only frustrate and harden the hearts of the believers who do not come to understand this mystery. They will never understand why the promises of God are not being experienced.

Even though the focal point of the gospel is centered around the good news of Jesus, we sometimes forget that in its most complete sense, it is the Gospel of the Kingdom. Every aspect of the good news is only perceivable within the context of the Kingdom. If our hearts are not teachable, open and fully surrendered to Jesus as Lord, we will ignore His teaching about the Kingdom, live mediocre lives and turn the glorious gospel into a foolish religion that has no power.

In pursuit of Kingdom living, we look for that which is invisible to the natural mind. Seeing the invisible is what sustained the Apostle Paul in the extreme persecutions he repeatedly encountered. It is what gave Moses and all the Old Testament saints the courage to face kings, lions, and the sword and still overcome. On the other hand, when believers perceive and enter into their inheritance of the Kingdom of God, they discover all the resources of heaven at their disposal.

Like the religious leaders of Jesus's day, we insist that being able to properly quote a verse or debate doctrine means we know the truth. This is, at its best, a form of self-deception. We conveniently forget, when the Bible uses the word know it is talking about experiencing. In other words, we do not know what we are not experiencing. Quoting scriptures about peace is a poor substitute for living in peace. So it is with all the promises: we can have talk or power. The Kingdom of God is not in word, but in power, (1 Cor. 4:20, KJV). Jesus warned the one thing that would keep us blind is to insist that we see (John 9:41, NASB). Any time our lives are not consistently functioning in the realm of abundant life, we must admit to ourselves, "There is something I am not seeing. I may know the information, but I am not experiencing the truth!"

So how do we resolve the mystery? How do we see what cannot be seen? How do we turn lifeless information into Words of life? How do we make a journey into a realm into which no man can lead us? It is all about a certain kind of attitude, starting with the choice to surrender to Jesus as Lord, make ourselves disciples and pursue the same quality of life as Jesus taught and lived. Remember, the one prerequisite for making this journey is a teachable (repentant) heart that is ready to be taught of the Lord.

In the Hebrew alphabet, every letter has its own individual definition. These definitions are based on the original Hebrew alphabet which was a series of pictures conveying specific ideas. Knowing the meanings of these letters brings incredible depth to the words. One very unique letter is the open MEM. The MEM originally looked like the top of our letter "M" and produced the same sound, The top of the MEM looked like waves because it represented water. In the ancient world, water has always represented a mystery, e.g., water is the most pliable and adaptable natural element, but it is also the most powerful. Like the heart, water takes on the shape of the vessel that holds it. The MEM represents God's revealed knowledge. The shape of the letter is a picture of God pouring knowledge on to the earth for all men, in the form of His written Word.

Since the MEM also represents water, we understand how it can be seen from various angles, whether from the shore or from a boat. If our view of the water is incredibly limited, we can only guess at what lies in its depths. We may be right, or we may be wrong; either way, we have never seen it for ourselves. We could, however, dive into the water and discover by personal experience the wonders are hidden beneath the surface.

Another unique letter is called a closed MEM, which represents secret or private knowledge. God's Word is revealed to us in such a way that we understand how to apply it to our present circumstances. It is the Holy Spirit who teaches us how to practically apply truth so that it brings life. While this knowledge is available to all, it is an exchange that only happens in heart-to-heart intimacy.

Only when we believe God's revealed Word through the open MEM (revealed knowledge) can we expect to enter into an intimacy where He personally instructs how to apply it. To make light of God's Word, interpret it irresponsibly, deny it or reject it, is to call God a liar. No one has intimacy with someone they do not trust. While God wants to share in intimacy with all of His children, not all of His children desire or are willing to hear Him. To do so, would reveal personal agendas and selfish motives.

In the interpretation and understanding of the Word of God, there is a final element. The final filter through which we must seek to understand is personal application. Those who simply want the information create intellectual interpretations of God's Word usually bent to their own preferences and agendas. Believers committed to being disciples want to understand how it applies in real life. Pharisaical believers want to have the "right" doctrine for the purpose of being right. Disciples, on the other hand, want to know the interpretation so they can know how to live and will ultimately unravel the mystery. Every step of learning, renewing the mind and transformation takes them to a new level of insight for life application.

The ancient Hebrews said there are 50 faces to the Torah; in other words, God's Word is so rich and deep there is always more than one way to understand it. All of these ways nevertheless, cannot violate His names. Even more important for New Covenant believers is that they cannot be incongruent with the life, teaching, death, burial, and resurrection of Jesus; therefore, every Word of God must be interpreted and applied from the motive of love. Then, and only then, can we discover our personal life application. Remember, the Word of God is absolute, but the application is variable.

A mystery unfolds through a process of initiations and growing in a particular truth. When that truth is accepted, believed and applied to our lives, we finally understand it. From that new insight, we naturally see the next step of our growth, which then repeats the same process. There is no end to discovering and experiencing the *"… width and length and height and depth of … the love of Christ which far passes knowledge, that you may be filled with all the fullness of God."* (Eph 3:18-19, AMP)

HeartWork

Read This Aloud Before Every HeartWork Session: The Kingdom of God is internal. HeartWork is designed to remove any internal obstacles that prevent me from entering the realm where I experience Heaven on Earth!

Honestly answer the following questions. When needed, give prayerful attention to any area that needs to be reconciled.

1. Do I qualify every Word of God by His names, the life, teaching, death, burial, and resurrection of Jesus as applied from God's definition of love?

2. Will I give up all personal agendas and seek the righteousness of God?

3. Am I a disciple, searching for how to live as Jesus taught and modeled?

4. Do I accept the validity of God's Word as taught by Jesus?

CHAPTER 9

The Walk of Faith

Faith is not blind, faith is when we see more clearly than ever before!

I have heard it said, the Old Covenant is based on works, but the New Covenant is based on faith. At some point in my early walk with God, I made those same statements. Sadly, I was simply repeating what I had been taught. The more I studied the scripture the more I realized this statement was incredibly inaccurate and opposed Scripture.

As the writer of Hebrews says, *"But without faith it is impossible to please Him [God] ...."* (Heb. 11:6, KJV) The word please can mean: "to be by fulling pleasing, to be fully agreeable" or "to be well-pleasing, to take pleasure in," and "to walk as is well-pleasing." The dimensions of this word have incredible ramifications. In the absence of faith, God is not pleased, we are not in harmony with God nor can we find pleasure in what we do for God; therefore, our actions will never be as they should. Believers who have the intention of being pleasing to God, not in the form of works-righteousness, but in the context of a loving relationship, cannot do so apart from faith.

While doing my undergraduate studies in theology, I passed many nights searching the Scripture to understand faith. The more I sought to understand, the more I found modern, self-contradictory teachings about faith, a random accumulation of partial truths, and formulas for legalistic ritualism. Like so many modern teachings, faith was not, however, hard to understand once I repented (changed my mind) by surrendering the modern definition I had accepted, which actually opposed the word as it was used in the original languages.

Hebrews 11:1 (KJV) says, *"Now faith is ... the evidence of things not seen."* If we stop there, we reach the illogical, mystical conclusion that faith is blind–a leap into the unknown. Those concepts, although embraced by religion, are in complete contradiction to what the word means and how it is used in Scripture. Faith sees with the eyes of our heart, not the eyes connected to our brain. Our natural eyes are connected to our brain, where it interprets what is seen. The eyes of our heart, on the other hand, send signals to the heart which are interpreted by the beliefs of the heart.

" ... [W]alk[ing] by faith, not by sight" (2 Cor. 5:7, KJV) is where our religious teaching kicks into overdrive, telling us that faith is blind, to just shut our eyes and take a leap of faith. This is an absurd concept because faith is not blind at all. Faith clearly sees what the natural mind or the unbelieving heart cannot see. Thayer's Greek Lexicon says the word sight is clearly speaking of outward appearance.

The Greek indicates that faith is being sure, fully persuaded and immovable. The deep assurance of faith is not blind; in actuality, it perceives God quite clearly, based on His testimony of Himself. To know and trust His character means we can know and trust His promises. As a new believer reading the Gospel of Matthew, I was continually struck by the prophecies that were fulfilled concerning the life, death, and resurrection of Jesus. Seeing God's trustworthiness to fulfill His every Word was monumental to establishing my faith. Words He had uttered thousands of years prior came to pass when and how He had foretold them with incredible accuracy.

In the Hebrew, the words truth and faithful originate from the same root word. This implies that if it is truth, God is faithful to it, and He is always faithful to His truth. He never changes, and no man can make Him change. Faith is built from discovering how faithful God is to His Word, basing that faithfulness on His character and nature as proven through thousands of years of recorded history and as modeled by the life, teaching, and resurrection of Jesus.

Jesus took a handful of common men and women who had lived under the yoke of oppressive, religious legalism, and by finding freedom in Him, they turned the world upside down. The reason they withstood such violent persecution was twofold: first, they knew the Scriptures; therefore, they understood the references and basis from which Jesus taught. Their faith was built on the objective proof of God's Word. Their subjective interaction with God, through the Lord Jesus, caused them to believe and experience truth in their own lives.

They experienced the power of Kingdom living. In their hearts, they experienced righteousness, peace, and joy in the Holy Spirit. Their beliefs and emotions were not based on external factors, making them strong in the Lord and in the power of His might. They believed and experienced the promises internally even when they were actively laying down their lives.

People who do not know Scripture have absolutely no basis for this kind of stability; they are those in whom, whether from unbelief or simply never learning the truth, the Word has never taken root in their heart. They cannot, as a result, inherit the Kingdom, although it has been freely offered. All three core factors for immovable faith must be present at the same time if we are to enter in and live this Kingdom life: quality seed, quality soil, and nurturing for growth.

The second factor that caused the disciples to turn the world upside down while withstanding unthinkable persecution was their personal, intimate involvement with God through the Lord Jesus after His resurrection. When Scripture is not the basis for our knowledge of God, we have nothing through which the Holy Spirit can operate. We cannot attempt to know God through our pastor, our favorite doctrines or the testimonies of others.

The carnal (natural) mind thinks, "If I understand it, I will believe it." Such an egocentric approach is equivalent to putting God on trial where He has to prove His truthfulness. It is like saying, "Your Word is not true until it meets my criteria." This is exactly what Israel did in the wilderness. They tested God By putting Him on trial and convicting Him of being untrustworthy, thereby justifying their unbelief and disobedience. Trust based on intellectual or subjective persuasion can be changed with another, more compelling intellectual persuasion. This type of trust is not faith in God, but faith in our intellectualism.

Hebrews 11:3 (NASB) tells us, *"By faith we understand ...."* The mind thinks when we understand it, then we can believe it, which means as our own god we determine truth by our own standards, opinions, and experiences. The heart, however, only understands after it believes. Again, this is not blind faith but rather a believing that comes from a clear knowledge of Scripture, through a teachable heart open to the Holy Spirit based on a deeply intimate relationship with God. Once we believe, our perception changes; and then the eyes of our heart see and perceive, and the ears of our heart hear and understand.

Sadly, for the last 50 years, faith has been taught as trusting in what God will do more than knowing and trusting who God is. From that perspective alone, we have been taught all manner of ways to convince ourselves that the promise is ours. While these processes are not entirely wrong or evil, trusting for the promise apart from knowing and trusting in the promise-maker is utterly backward.

Every challenge in this life can be faced as an overcomer, based on our absolute knowledge and confidence in the written Word of God, His consistent, loving, and generous nature and His unlimited resources. Trusting God for small things is comparable to confidently asking a friend for five dollars as opposed to five thousand dollars. The amount for which we can confidently trust to ask is based on the depth of the relationship and the resources of the friend.

Believing God to provide His resources for our situation apart from a deep personal relationship would be like asking a stranger for a large sum of money just because that person is wealthy. It is a shot in the dark. Likewise, faith in what God will do, apart from trust (faith) in His character through personal intimacy, is a shot in the dark.

HeartWork

Read This Aloud Before Every HeartWork Session: The Kingdom of God is internal. HeartWork is designed to remove any internal obstacles that prevent me from entering the realm where I experience Heaven on Earth!

Read and consider each of the following questions before moving on to the next chapter.

1. What am I doing right now to grow in my knowledge and relationship with God?

2. Do I really know God well enough to be confident in His desire to use His resources to better my life?

3. How many promises of God do I know by heart?

4. Do I have a scriptural basis for knowing that the promise for this situation belongs to me?

CHAPTER 10

Seeing the End from the Beginning

Foresight gives us the power to choose the future we desire!

In Mark 11:22 (KJV), Jesus tells us to *"have faith in God."* Some theologians say this phrase implies that the believer should have the same kind of faith God has. Religion would reject such a thing as impossible, but God is our model for everything; and, after all, we are created in His likeness and image. When Jesus came to earth, He showed us exactly what it looks like for man to operate in faith the same way God does.

When God created the universe, He established the model for operating in faith. God actually followed the exact pattern Jesus taught in Mark 11:23: He conceived something in His heart, spoke faith-filled words and did not waver–the perfect biblical model for faith!

In the Book of Genesis, we have the repeated statement, *"Then God said, let there be ... "* The following statements usually occurred in some shape, form or fashion, *"... and it was so."* The final part of the sequence of statements was, *"... and it was good!"*

In the Hebrew, there are different words from which we translate "said" or "to speak." One places the emphasis on speaking, while the other places the emphasis on speaking what has been conceived and developed in the heart. The word used when God created the universe is a word that emphasizes the fact that all He spoke was first conceived in His heart!

For years believers have tried to operate faith-based on speaking with little to no emphasis on having first conceived it in our heart. The faith principle taught was to simply believe that what one said would come to pass. It was sort of faith in your faith. I'm not saying this is entirely wrong, but it isn't really faith in God.

A major component is operating faith in God, is rooted in he to first principles faith: 1) faith in the creation account just as it is in the Bible, and 2) faith in the fact that man is created in the likeness and image of God. The moment, we deviate or contradict any of the principle embodied in those two realities, we are no longer in faith. Equally important, is when we take actions because we believe those accounts.

Because we believe we are created in the likeness and image of God, we know our operation of faith should be identical to God's. Our faith is in the way God created us, and they way He modeled faith; it's faith in God personally, faith in His Word and faith in His process! So let's look a little deeper into God's process.

First, God formulated the outcome He desired. Faith always sees, perceived, i.e. knows and declares the end from the beginning, Is. 46:10. We have the idea that God simply blurted out what He wanted to be created, spoke the words, in a very general way, and the earth, solar system, planets, galaxies, and all their interactions simply appeared. But it was far more specific and deliberate than that!

Every second of every day there are millions of interaction between the cells of the body. These are dependent upon the environment on planet earth, which is reliant upon the billions of interactions between the planets in our solar system, which rely on our galaxy, which is dependent on other galaxies ad infinitum. Every moment there are trillions and trillions of interactions, based on mathematical formulas, all of which God had to know and apply to create a universe that works so perfectly to provide a unique environment on planet earth to sustain human life.

Every creative word He spoke was with delivered with the absolute assurance of it occurring. In fact, in His heart, there was no possibility they would not create precisely what He intended. Since God impregnated the universe with immutable laws, it seems that we do not have to be as detailed in our creative process. By His ultimate creation, all the laws are in place to give creative potential to the end we see and believe, without the need to know every detail of how it needs to happen.

Once this is done, all that's left is don't doubt. Doubt is in the continuum of wavering. Once we have believed and set the process of faith to work, far too often we change our focus from the end we have seen, spoken and perceive in our heart to a negative outcome. While in faith, we have planted the seed of God's Word into our heart, but when we shift our focus to another outcome, we actually begin to fill our heart with other seed. If this continues, the bad seed will choke out the good seed.

The Apostle Peter provides great insight into this process when he says we are all receiving the goal of our faith. Due to a limited definition of salvation, some tend only to apply this to the new birth. But the scope of "salvation" is massive. Salvation of our soul is when we personally experience every aspect of salvation: saved, healed, delivered, blessed, prospered, protected, set apart, and etc. This is the life of God, legally given to us through Jesus, transitioned into our real-life experience. But it only happens when that is the goal and intention of our faith.

The majority of believers, I've personally counseled, are afraid to determine a clear intention or goal about the outcome of their faith. They are trapped in the religious, unscriptural quagmire of, "I'm not sure if it's God's will." They act as if, God is making the decision about every prayer individually. The truth is, God has made His will abundantly clear. If we are in Christ, we are free from the curse of the law (Gal 3:13); every promise God has ever made to anyone is yes for us (2 Cor 1:20); we are qualified to be partakers in the inheritance (Col 1:12). If Jesus settled it through His death, burial, and resurrection, there nothing else we need to know.

One of the first core factors of faith is we are created in the likeness and image of God. Therefore, how God operates is how we operate. The way God walks in faith is the way we walk in faith. We're not simply placing faith in our faith. The root of our faith is how we were created; we function like God functions; everything Jesus accomplished through the cross is for everyone who is in Christ! Those who believe these truths, choose the promise of God; they have faith in the finished work of Jesus, and they exercise faith just as God did at creation, and as Jesus taught on earth.

Jesus spoke in an Aramaic dialect, not Greek. When the scriptures were written in Greek, they were often words that had no equal in the Greek; therefore phrases sometimes replaced words; occasionally entire concepts were lost. When Jesus stood in the boat with the disciples addressing the storm, He had no need to pray. He knew God was good and only good. He knew God's Word and His name; therefore it was not the will of God for Him and His disciples to die. In the Greek, it states that He said, "Peace be still!" Which makes sense. But in the Aramaic, He said, "Surrender to the will of God!"[1] When we believe the Scripture, there's nothing to pray about.

The third law of faith is rooted in the fact that God gave us dominion on planet earth. It is we, the believers who establish God's will on planet earth. That can only happen, however, when we believe who God is and who we are in Him.

When the wind and the waves calmed, they were in harmony with the will of God. That's our role as believers: we bring our lives and planet earth back in harmony by using our faith. In Genesis when God would speak, things would happen, and it would say "It's good," this words embodies more than a single ad-

1   Based on the actual Hebrew language. Chaim Bentorah ChaimBentorah.com

jective. The word "good" in Hebrew nearly always presents the idea if harmony. In other words what God created was in harmony with His intention, i.e., with that which He conceived in His heart before He spoke.

When we create a clear picture or end result in our heart, which is in harmony with the finished work of Jesus, apply the God kind of faith, the end result will be good. It will be in harmony with the Word of God and with that which we saw and declared from the beginning.

HeartWork

Read This Aloud Before Every HeartWork Session: The Kingdom of God is internal. HeartWork is designed to remove any internal obstacles that prevent me from entering the realm where I experience Heaven on Earth!

1. What decisions are you presently trying to make?

2. Identify the end result you desire.

3. As much as you can, conceptualize that end and how you will experience it.

4. Then consider the following questions.

    a. Do I know the outcome I desire is based on the promises of God?

    b. Am I confident I am qualified for this because I am in Christ?

5. Ponder, imagine or meditate the end you desire, when you see it clearly operate the faith of God.

    a. See it in your heart

    b. Speak it into existence

    c. Don't allow yourself to doubt

    d. Expect the outcome you have declared

CHAPTER 11

A Moral Kingdom

The hope of a good life is either poisoned or profited by our morals and ethics!

As much as anything the Kingdom of God is a realm wherein we choose to live in the same virtue as God. God repeatedly stated, *"Be holy for/as I am holy."* We are called to have the same character and nature, i.e. virtues as God. Jesus said we are the light of the world, we should look, behave, talk and function from the same values as God, who loves His enemies. Blesses those who curse Him, does good to those who hate Him, pray (intercede) for those who use and persecute Him.

Verse 44 tells us to do good to those who hate us. Chaim Bentorah, my Hebrew teacher states:

In the Northern dialect of Aramaic Jesus used the word tob which we render as good. Tob is identical to Hebrew word tov which means to be in harmony with God. In other words, let your response to the one who hates you be in harmony with God's response. God's response is one of love.[1]

Goodness not only puts our response in harmony with God, but it also creates the possibility that the individual may bring his or her life into harmony with God. After all, it is the goodness of God that draws people to repentance, Ro. 2:4.

In the previous passage, Jesus is not telling us how to earn our way into becom-

1 BENTORAH, CHAIM (2013-10-23). HEBREW WORD STUDY: A Hebrew Teacher Finds Rest in the Heart of God (p. 111). Trafford. Kindle Edition.

ing sons. It is telling us how to be sons who are actually like God and bringing His light into the world by acting in harmony with the true character and nature of God the Father.

Unfortunately, much of Christendom profoundly misunderstands why God wants us to be moral, virtuous people. With the advent of Catholicism Christianity became a predominantly works-based religion. The character of God was besmirched by the incorporation of paganistic concepts of Asceticism, Gnosticism, and Luciferianism into our beliefs about God. Morality and virtue was no longer our representation of God to the world, it became the standard whereby the church judged the world. It was believed to be the primary way we earned salvation. There was virtually no acknowledgment of how our character affected our heart our faith and the world.

God has always desired His people to embrace and value a virtuous life i,e, seek first the Kingdom of God and His righteousness. God called Israel and the church to represent Him on the earth. But we must represent Him as priests and Kings representing a holy God and a holy nation. The one characteristic that expresses holiness (uncommonness) more than any other is His love for His creation. He created us, He wants the best for us; and He provided the blueprint, i.e. the handbook for how to have a great life: peace in our heart, a unique quality of life and pure love for one another.

When God brought Israel out of Egypt, He established the model for the believer seeking the Kingdom. After being baptized into Christ the first goal of every believer should be to renew their mind. The renewing of the mind not only teaches us what to think but how to think in a way that always leads us down the path of life. The path of life is a path that always keeps us in harmony with God!

Mt. Sinai was the place where they renewed their mind. This is where they should have discovered God's value for loving one another, because eight of the ten commandments were about how we treat one another. God gave the Ten Commandments, the problem is we have no English equivalent to the actual Hebrew word. When we hear the word "commandment" we default to something we are being forced to do. Many believers only have a negative connotation of the commandments, as if they are difficult or burdensome.

In Hebrew, the word really isn't commandment at we think of it. It is something much more positive. One writer says the closest word we have that embodies the Hebrew is the "prescription." The commandments are prescriptions that heal our relationships, with God, self, and others. They are preventative in nature.

The Israelites much like many 21st century believers, after centuries of religious propaganda, embrace a pagan concept of God. He is a hard taskmaster, and the commandments were rules that He would enforce with a heavy hand. They have nothing to do with love, they are seen as laws we obey to earn favor and acceptance. However, more than any other concept God presents Himself as a loving Father. His command is used for the instruction of a father to a son[1] The Israelites never freed themselves from a slave mentality, and they never accepted God's testimony of Himself. Much of the church suffers the same malignancy: religion!

Slaves operate from the principles of the world's system: Egypt. Because the world is brutal we are justified to lie, cheat, steal or violate any of the commandments as a way to have "the good life." This is the mind of the carnal (natural) minded believer. They do not see how walking in love could ever get them what they desire. Many Christians who claim to walk in love are actually walking in Humanitarianism, which defines love wholly different and usually opposed to God's prescribed manner of walking in love. Therefore, walking in love, or what appears to be love, is only a means of manipulations; even while doing what they do in the name of God they are actually opposing God!

The believer who has surrendered to Lordship and chose to become a disciple, may not understand how it all works, but they very quickly realize, walking in God's love must be their highest personal goal. The Apostle John said, *"By this, we know that we love the children of God, when we love God and keep His commandments. For this is the love of God, that we keep His commandments. And His commandments are not burdensome."* 1 John 5:2-4.

Lest anyone misunderstand or twist my words, I must point out: first and foremost we are not under the law we are under grace. But the commandments are God's prescription for walking love. Jesus taught, walking in God's definition of love must be our highest goal. Fortunately, we have the Holy Spirit who has transformed our nature and give us a strength the Bible calls grace. Grace makes us able to walk in love. Grace is God's power, strength, and capacity which works from the heart of the believer.

The born again believer can walk in love if he or she desires; the question is, do they trust God's teaching about love or will they continue in the world's system, after being freed from sin? This is the Christian who wanders in the wilderness. They are the ones who testify how much harder life is now that they are "Christian". Like the mixed multitude of Israel, these are the ones that longingly look back to Egypt desiring the pleasures of sin, because they do not trust God enough to follow Him into the Kingdom

If Israel had trusted and followed God's they would have never wandered in the wilderness. In just a few weeks they could have entered Canaan. They would have probably seen more incredible miracles than have ever been witnessed. After all, only by God's miraculous power could a group of slaves with no army conquer the fiercest nations on the earth.

---

1   from Theological Wordbook of the Old Testament. Copyright © 1980 by The Moody Bible Institute of Chicago. All rights reserved. Used by permission.

They would have become the most just, loving nation in the world. By following His commands, there would have never been political and religious oppression. The rich could never have monopolized the poor. They had the best civil laws for women, immigrants, slaves, and citizens in the world. Their virtue would have been their reputation in the world. All the nations of the earth would have desired the peace and power they had. All their enemy nations would have feared them because they would have seen the constant presence of God among them.

Nowhere does the New Testament do away with any of the commandments; instead it elevates them to a level that says they must be applied from the motive of love and they must be obeyed from your heart! Jesus, Paul, and the apostles thoroughly rejected the Talmud, the doctrine of the Pharisees, Sadducees and all other religious sects as the interpretation and application. Jesus is the definitive insight into interpreting and applying the Word of God.

Like the nation of Israel, we are called to live in a moral kingdom from our heart. Since the heart is the seat of our identity, our morality and ethics must be who we are, not simply what we do! This is where we enter into the paradox. Our morality isn't what gives us the right to the inheritance. That right comes because we are heirs of God and joint-heirs in Jesus. But our morality and ethics do determine if we can possess the inheritance.

In Lev 20:24 it says, *"You shall inherit their land, and I will give it to you to possess, a land flowing with milk and honey."* The land became Israel's possession because the Creator gave it to them. However, they had to walk with Him, by faith, obey His commandments as the absolute standard of love, relationships, civil and moral law, if they ever hoped to occupy it. The word "possess is synonymous with occupy. Just as an immoral, unethical Israel could not possess the inheritance God gave them, a Christian cannot occupy, i.e. possess the Kingdom of God.

Think about like this: every year people all across America win lotteries. These are people are convinced, if only they could get "ahead" their life would forever be different. When they win the lottery, they not only get ahead they become millionaires. You would think they would so value their new found wealth, they would carefully guard it. You would think they would protect the future they could have. But most don't! One statistic says on average they will be bankrupt in 3-5 years. In most cases, they will be worse off financially than before they won the lottery. It's like a Christian who is given his or her inheritance but doesn't have the character to hold on to it!

2 Peter 1:3 says God has called us to *glory and virtue.* Romans 8:29 says we are predestined to be *conformed to the likeness of Jesus.* Every epistle reaffirms the need for godly living! It seems there is little connection between the pain in our life and our lack of character and morals. It is the typical "mystic Christian faith:" I can stay the same and God can make everything in my life get better. I find few

believers that realize they are the source of all their problems. Salvation is about us changing from the inside out. The evidence and fruit of that transformation our quality of life!

The Apostle Paul expended incredible effort in Romans chapter six explaining, we are new creations, with a righteous nature, under grace; yet we still have the freedom to choose to yield to sin or righteousness. He reminds that the wages of sin are death for the believer just as they are for the nonbeliever. In Chapter seven he explains, even though we are righteous, we still have to deal with sin through the struggle that wars in our mind and members. But then in Romans chapter eight, He teaches us to yield to the Spirit, free from condemnation about our struggle and find victory through the grace of God. Many have twisted his words into a strange "sin is okay" doctrine, totally foreign to anything in the Old or New Testaments.

Paul tells us the Kingdom of God is righteousness, peace, and joy in the Holy Spirit. Again, they are not characteristics whereby one earns the kingdom. They are the fruit, the internal state, i.e. the naturally occurring phenomena of one living in this realm called the Kingdom of God. The believer who does not manifest righteousness: life as it should be in Jesus, peace: a tranquility which comes from experiencing access to God and His resources, and joy: the continual celebration of life with God, is not possessing the Kingdom of God! They've won the lottery, but they still live like broke, desperate poverty stricken fools! God cannot bring Zoe, i.e., God's quality of life, to a life of chaos, immoral or unethical pursuits. It's like putting ice in boiling water. It can only cool the temperature if you take the pot off the fire!

HeartWork

Read This Aloud Before Every HeartWork Session: The Kingdom of God is internal. HeartWork is designed to remove any internal obstacles that prevent me from entering the realm where I experience Heaven on Earth!

Take time to ponder, consider and reflect on the honest answers to these questions.

1. Do I fully believe and understand that I am the source of all my problems?

2. Do I fully believe and accept that no one outside of me changing will fill my heart with peace?

3. Am I fully committed to living a godly life marked by walking in love as God describes it?

4. Do I fully accept that God's commandments are the only basis for defining love?

5. Do I realize and accept it is beyond my natural strength to live this life to which God has called me?

6. Do I depend fully on the strength of God to make me able to live this life, in Christ, I have chosen?

CHAPTER 12

Check the Fruit

If you don't like what's growing in the garden, plant different seeds!

Kingdom living is a commitment to personal responsibility and individual choice! Historically, the Hebrew people seemed to recognize the first two laws of faith clearly: God created the universe exactly as described in the Bible, and He created man in His likeness and image, very specifically implying man has a free will which God will never violate

Personal choice and responsibility are strikingly present in every book of the Bible. We choose life or death, blessing or cursing; we choose to hold to painful offenses or send them away. God never violates our choices. When we refuse to choose, we are left to the natural progression of the world which always tends to death. It is this very issue of personal choice and responsibility that the majority of Christian groups simply refuse to accept.

When we do not accept and follow this undergirding principle, we conjure up all manner mystical concepts of God. In fact, it makes it impossible to operate in Kingdom principles, since all Kingdom principles rely on personal choice. In nearly a half-century of personal ministry and counseling the majority of believers, genuinely seeking God are suffering because they are ignoring: the finished work of Jesus; they are asking questions God already answered; they're asking God to do what He has already done, or they are waiting for God to do their part!

Many people will challenge the responsibility of choice with the accusation, "You're leaving God out. You've got to wait until you know His will." As spiritual and humble as that sounds it is just the opposite. When we know the new covenant provision and promises, we realize God has already made His choices and done all of His part of the process. That's why it is called "the finished work of Jesus."

His part is finished ours is not! We still must make our own decisions to receive and participate in what God is doing. That decision is a decision of trust (faith). The one who does not trust is continually going back to God the, "Is your promise still good? Is it really good for me? Is there anything else I need to know?" The person who trusts God knows: He does not change; He is always true to His promise; there's nothing left for Him to do! The entire process, including the struggles and the traps, is laid out in Israel's History from Egypt to being expelled from the Kingdom, as a type of what God is promising us. The fulfillment is in Jesus!

The key is to faith (trust) is believing God's testimony about Himself. By believing on Jesus as Lord, we were baptized into the spiritual body of Christ. When Jesus rose from the dead, God sealed the covenant of peace with Him, in His blood, and he obtained the inheritance of the Kingdom. Since we are in Him, we share in His inheritance; therefore, all the promises God has ever made are ours (2 Cor. 1:20). Trusting that our inheritance is secure in Christ is our absolute assurance that our desires can and will be fulfilled without the sacrifice of our virtue. We can walk with God and have our desires fulfilled in a godly manner that does not bring death, destruction, or pain to us or to the world around us.

In the Garden, man declared independence from God. The abandoning of Adam's faith expressed that man no longer desired to know good and evil based on God's Word and Wisdom. Instead, he decided to make that determination independent of God. In other words, man's declaration to God was, "I don't trust you; I trust me!" Hence, our concepts of good and evil may play a major role in our failure to understand the significance of such a decision. Good and evil go far beyond the scope of whether or not something is sinful. Some say this phrase means: from one extreme to the other and everything in between. The words good and evil are not merely concepts of sin and righteousness; they more aptly indicate the capacity to determine for oneself the outcome of every decision.

The concept of evil or wicked refers to that which causes pain, misery, distress, unpleasantness, displeasure, injury, misery, anything which is harmful, sorrow, or defeat. In the Hebrew, the word evil or wicked presents the concept of bending the path, corrupting our consciousness, and bringing us to a turning point. In the Greek it is something that leads to malignancy and is related to the words prison, cry, scatter, and sword. The word for good is the very opposite of evil, meaning pleasant, good, prosperous, pleasing, virtuous, healthy, the right timing, honorable, moral, praiseworthy, and more.

The word good in Hebrew lends itself to the concept of harmony with God and the word bent, or crooked presents the idea of disharmony. In Psalms and Proverbs, the King James Version of the word crooked or bent is usually translated as froward. Psalm 101:4 says, *"A froward (crooked) heart shall depart from me: I will not know a wicked person."* He who has a heart that is not in harmony with God and His word will continually, by degrees depart from God, even while the name of God is on his or her lips, their hearts are far from Him!

Possibly the greatest tragedy in real life is to him who does not have he loses even what he has. That very lack dominating our heart takes from us what little we do have and keeps taking until it brings us to emotional and ultimately physical death. When we understand the dichotomy of good and evil, we understand how a crooked, or wicked, heart has so corrupted our understanding that we neither choose the good nor can we even find it. The way we see and process information is out of harmony with God, thus, the Proverb: *"He that hath a froward (crooked) heart findeth no good."* 17:20

Truth is light, and light makes us able to see, perceive, and understand what is really occurring in any situation. But when light bends, it changes colors. Likewise, when the light of God's truth attempts to shine into a crooked heart, the light is bent to the preferences, deceptions, and lusts. It no longer makes the path of life clear to the observer but rather distorts; but it makes the way of death seem right, logical and good!

Another, lesser known concept of the word evil is an unrealistic optimism. A crooked heart is convinced that sin has no derogatory effect on our lives. We really believe we can take hot coals into our laps and not be burned (Pro. 6:27). Our incapability for Kingdom living is not a punishment of God, but rather the result of choosing the way of death because we believe it is the better way to obtain our desires. It is exactly as Jesus said, *"to him who has not, even what he thinks he has is taken away."* (Luke 8:18)

A crooked heart does not consider the outcome of its ways (Pro. 14:8) nor factor them into the equation of life. In fact, I have talked to thousands of people who will insist, I am praying and seeking God, but nothing is working. The one thing they are not doing is changing the basis from which they are making their decisions. The NLT probably says it best: *"People ruin their lives by their own foolishness."* (Prov. 19:3) We want to ignore God's warnings and then blame God for the outcome. This generation seems to have lost any correlation between their, beliefs, behavior and the dysfunction in their lives!

God is always attempting to warn us when life is taking us in a destructive direction. So when everything is falling apart, we have to consider our own ways. This is not an introspective witch hunt nor does it necessitate blaming ourselves or passing personal judgments. It is recognizing that God tells us how to have the best in life; our choices and behavior merely reveal the object of our faith—either ourselves or God. If our behavior reveals a lack of trust for God, all we have to do is repent. Otherwise, we can never find the doorway into the Kingdom.

One of the major factors of prayer is self-assessment. This is not personal condemnation; it is not unhealthy self-searching. It is simply looking at our life and asking a question. Since I'm a child of God, in Jesus, delivered from the curse, qualified for all the promises is this how my life should be?

> *Consider your ways! You have sown much, and bring in little; You eat, but do not have enough; You drink, but you are not filled with drink; You clothe yourselves, but no one is warm; And he who earns wages, Earns wages to put into a bag with holes."* (Hag. 1:5-6). *"Consider her ways and be wise.* (Prov. 6:6)

Jeremiah 6:16 provides incredibly wise and simple instructions when we find ourselves standing at a crossroads: choose the way that leads to rest, peace, and harmony with God. In every decision, we make a choice concerning which path we will take. The outcome is the result of the choice; the choice is the expression of our heart beliefs. If we trust God and His Word we can see the end from the beginning. We may not know all the specifics of how bad or good things will become, but we can know for sure whether the end will be good or bad, i.e. life or death!

HeartWork

Read This Aloud Before Every HeartWork Session: The Kingdom of God is internal. HeartWork is designed to remove any internal obstacles that prevent me from entering the realm where I experience Heaven on Earth!

As you consider the follow questions, do not become introspective, negative of self-judgmental. Simply consider the quality of your life and honestly answer these questions. Because I am a Child of the Creator; I have been given all things that pertain unto life and godliness, I am delivered from the curse and all the promises are yes for me, Is this reflected in my:

1. Emotional health?

2. Personal relationships?

3. Finances?

4. Physical health?

5. And peace of mind?

Do not be concerned if you answered "no" to any or all of these. You are reading this book to discover how to enter into Kingdom living! Continue making the journey. Refuse to give up all that Jesus died to give you!

CHAPTER 13

The Silent Killer

Indecision is an incurable disease

God created us with a unique capacity to make decisions. Once we make a decision, all our internal resources begin to work synergistically to fulfill that decision. Prov 29:18 says, *"Where there is no vision, the people perish."* While there are many concepts embedded in this verse, it's not too much of a stretch to apply this to personal vision.

One translation says these people *cast off restraint*, another says they *run wild*! The straightest translation points out that this is talking about people whose vision, i.e., perception is not based on the Word of God, will, in fact, run wild! In our personal lives, this is true in a more general sense! People who have no defined life goal, short-range target or clear-cut intention are like a ship without a rudder! They are tossed to and fro based on the winds of life.

As a counselor, I have seen people's emotional and physical energy change simply because they made a decision. This also has a profound effect on our mental capacities. Great idea seldom to come to anyone who is not searching for something. It's the people knocking who have doors of opportunity swing open before them. It is those who are searching that find the incredible treasures of life.

All those treasures and opportunities are always there, the problem is, however, those who are passively waiting for God to make the decisions, He tells us to make can't see them. Ecclesiastes 9:1, points out that success isn't about skill or intelligence as much as it is about time and change which comes to all men. Both these words "time and chance" have a strong emphasis on perception. Therefore, it is saying, success or good outcomes are present for everyone; some people see and seize the opportunity others never notice and let it go by!

People of faith believe there is a spiritual city (realm) whose builder and maker is God! They know and believe Canaan was not the ultimate "rest" God promised to Israel. They know there is a Kingdom only perceivable to the heart of faith. People of faith are not afraid to trust God. They need no additional signs; they don't need to lay out a "fleece." The testimony of Jesus raised from the dead is all the evidence they need.

Sadly, there are those who have just enough of God they can't enjoy the world and just enough of the world they can't enjoy God. They languish in the nether-world of indecision. They are weighted down with information they are afraid to act on. Like the mixed multitudes of Israel, they wanted out of slavery enough to follow God out of Egypt, they didn't trust God enough to enter into the Kingdom, so they are doomed to wander in the wilderness torment by promises greater than their trust for God!

Medical doctors call high blood pressure the silent killer. In the spiritual, physical and emotional realm, indecision is our silent killer. Because indecision doesn't appear to be an active step, it seems harmless. However, indecision is, in fact, an active statement of unbelief. It is a statement of fact: God I do not trust you or you Word enough to actually take any action. This falls into the realm of dead works, Ja. 2:20.

James' teachings are rejected by many who fail to understand the nature of faith. All actions or inactions are, actually, a statement of what we believe. It is the outward expression, i.e., the fruit of our faith. In both the Old and the New Testaments believing and obeying are pretty much synonymous. James teachings are based on Jesus teaching in Matthew 7:21-27. Jesus begins this passage with, *"Not everyone who says to Me, 'Lord, Lord,' shall enter the kingdom of heaven, but he who does the will of My Father in heaven."* (Matt 7:21) In these verses, He compares the fate of those who hear and apply His Word with those who hear and do not apply!

Many who do not apply Truth feel they are in a safe zone, they are not actively obeying or disobeying. Some get stuck in those deadly place because they need some greater proof than the resurrection of Jesus. Others are double-minded; they can't make up their mind what they do or do not believe. This is a deception if we are not seeking to apply God's Word it is our testimony that we do not believe God Word.

The nation of Israel, and the consequences of their wavering, which is our example for entering the Kingdom, was the poster child for a double mind! A double-minded, person is unstable in all their ways, i.e., in every part of his or her life, Ja. 1:8! The double-minded shift from one opinion to another, one point of view to another. On their journey from Egypt to Canaan, Israel continuously shifted from believing they could, to believing they couldn't.

This kind of shifting is characteristic of the person attempting to trust God on a case by case situation. It's like trying to trust the promise of someone you do not know very well. Every time they promise to do something you evaluate it. You don't know them well enough to be sure they'll do what they say; thus the size of the promise becomes the pivotal point of trust or non-trust! We actually project our character onto God as a way to judge Him. If the promise is something bigger than I can understand, or greater than what I would do for another, I won't believe the promise. If the promise is not too great, something I would easily do for someone, I'm willing to believe it.

This mentality results in putting the person who makes the promise on trial with each new promise. "I know you've already done that for me, but I don't know if you will really do this!" The Psalmist and the writer of Hebrews tell us Israel put God on trial, passed a judgment that He was not trustworthy, which resulted in limiting what God could do in their lives, 78:41. When they limited God, they forgot all the promises He had kept. They succumbed to temptation, to disbelieve God. Since they could only enter the Promised Land and conquer all their enemies by God's power, this unbelief rendered it impossible for them to enter into the promise. Then they blamed God for not keeping His promise!

Unbelief drags down the stony path of temptation. *Temptation* is anything that causes us to feel tested, tried, scrutinized, makes us strain or strive. Temptations emerge when we have legitimate, healthy desires but do not trust they can be fulfilled God's way, within the ethical, moral and godly parameters consistent with His character and nature. When we don't trust God's way or His character, as revealed by His Word, we turn to something we trust more than God. Whatever we turn away from God, it will be toward that which we learned from the world's system. Egypt is a type of the world's system. The *world's system* is any philosophical approach to life, whether secular or religious, that offers us what God has promised, apart from walking in His character and wisdom.

When Moses was on the mountain getting the commandments from God, the children of Israel fell into temptation. Temptation starts from legitimate needs and desires. Moses had stayed on the mountain so long they feared he had been killed by God. Moses was the one they looked to for leadership and survival. They had legitimate questions about how they would survive in the wilderness without Moses: where would they get food, water, and protection from the nations who sought to destroy them.

The problem is never our desires; no natural need or desire is inherently sinful. God is not only ready and willing to meet our desires and fulfill our needs, He has also already done so, through Jesus! But when we do not trust God as our source, when unbelief is present, temptation entices us to turn to something we trust more than we trust God. It is the determination of the knowledge of good and evil: our judgment, apart from God. Israel made a golden calf. Why? That was something they learned in Egypt! We justify our 21st Century paganism based on the fact that we didn't worship something as overtly idolatrous as a golden calf. But we did turn to another God: self!

Natural intelligence or desires are not evil; The desired to feel safe, the desire for provision, even the desire to succeed is not wrong. When, however, in pursuit of those desires we exalt our ideas above the Word of God, just like Adam eating from the tree… we begin to die. We put misplaced trust in what we learned in the world's system; we believe that system can give us what God offers, but without God! Those who trust in God's goodness and have not succumbed to religious perversion will turn to God and His Word to find the path that not only leads to the fulfillment of our needs and desires but causes us to stay deeply connected to God.

In 1 Kings 18:21, the prophet of Elijah taunted the unbelieving children of Israel with these words, *"How long will you waver between two opinions? If the Lord is God, follow him; but if Baal is God, follow him."* Maybe it's time we get "all in" with God. Don't wait for things to "change internally" before you make your decision. When you make your decision, things we internally change. Don't wait until you understand to make your decision to fully trust and follow God; when you believe and make a decision, your understanding will come.

Consider praying this: *Jesus, I believe God raised you from the dead, conquering all the curse, all that stood against me. I am in you, I am one with you; all that is yours is mine. I refuse to remain stuck in indecision. Bring me to the place where I see you as my source in all situations.*

HeartWork

Read This Aloud Before Every HeartWork Session: The Kingdom of God is internal. HeartWork is designed to remove any internal obstacles that prevent me from entering the realm where I experience Heaven on Earth!

1. Am I stuck in indecision?

2. Do I know enough of the promises of God that pertain to my need to actually trust God?

3. Because I believe on the resurrected Jesus, I believe Jesus conquered this problem on the cross.

4. Even though I am not fully convinced, I choose to trust God and invite Him to bring me to a place of faith!

CHAPTER 14

Pain and Pleasure

The one place no one wants to look to solve their problems is inward!

When we walk with God, we are not only seeking to believe in and experience a way of life better than anything we can imagine, but we are also seeking to live in a way that contradicts everything we've been taught. When we truly intend to experience the quality of life Jesus offers, we must renew our minds at every level of our life experience.

Renewing the mind includes two dimensions: what we think and how we interpret. An expert of the Law came to Jesus and asked, "what must I do to inherit eternal life." It is at this point, many believers would launch into their personal opinions concerning eternal life, usually making no reference to Scripture. When a person's response to a question that requires proper information, is not based on scripture it is highly possible, that person hasn't renewed their mind. Likewise, when asked a question concerning interpretation and application, if the person doesn't base their response on the life, teaching, death, burial, and resurrection of Jesus, not only is it doubtful they have renewed their mind, it is questionable if they actually embrace Jesus as Lord!

Since man rebelled against God, one of his greatest fears is the unknown. After all, Adam ultimately chose to live by his own knowledge and interpretation of good and evil rather than trusting God's love and wisdom. Similarly, we are uncomfortable walking an unknown path even when that path can lead to something enjoyable. The unknown makes us unsure if it will be a chaotic, hurtful (evil) experience or a pleasant, enjoyable (good) experience; therefore, it is in our inherent nature to avoid and even flee from the unknown. At the core of the fear of the unknown is our desire to be a god unto ourselves. We can't control what we do not know!

In the internal hierarchy, i.e., the process through which all decisions are made is our anticipation of pain and pleasure, pain and pleasure, i.e., good and evil. We were created to live in paradise with no physical, emotional or spiritual lack. Eden was God's will for man, and it was the environment that would sustain man forever. Because of the way man was created we are drawn toward that which we believe will bring us pleasure (good) we will withdraw from that which has the potential for pain (evil). This is why we were created with a nervous system: fight or flight.

We will risk the possibility of pain if the reward is certain and if it offers the expectation of enough pleasure. We will, on the other hand, most assuredly, forego any pleasure that is not gratifying enough to warrant the risk of pain. The life God is promising us is an unknown. Religion has made walking in love sound difficult and demeaning. Based on what we've heard and seen we have no reason to believe life can be that good. In fact, most religious input says Christian life should be bad; we should suffer to please God! Not only is that contrary to both Covenants, it is contrary to how man was created.

Since before the time of creation, man has been called to a life that is described by the Greek word *zoe*, which means *the quality of life possessed by the one who gives it.*[1] Thus, we are called to and promised the same quality of life that God Himself possesses. This *zoe* life, referred to by Jesus as the Kingdom of Heaven, represents all of God's heavenly resources, which he offers freely to us that we may literally experience heaven here on earth! The apostle Paul characterized kingdom living as righteousness, peace, and joy in the Holy Spirit, and according to Jesus, it is a life that is easy and light.

The promise of a better life is what attracts most people to Jesus initially, but then we become indoctrinated by religion. Rather than experiencing the freedom and love of the promise, religion instills obligation and fear. By twisting the truth, religion yanks the promise of Kingdom living right out of our hands under the pretense that pain and suffering are part of our Godly education, our Master's degree to growth and maturity in Christ. Yet, the fear this produces makes it impossible to wholeheartedly trust God, which is what He said is the very thing that pleases Him: faith! Moreover, those who desire the promises of God are condemned as selfish and carnal. In religion, all positive motivation for trusting and following God is destroyed. Once the character of God has been thoroughly assassinated beyond our ability to trust Him fully, the only motivation left to follow Him is induced by fear and obligation.

1   Biblico-Theological Lexicon of New Testament Greek, Hermann Cremer, D.D., T&T Clark, Edinburg, 1977 p 270-274, 721

Every human being has an inward awareness that life is supposed to be good. We crave it, we search for, but because of the negative influence of religion, we don't trust the only source of fulfilling that desire. But we don't stop looking, we just look in all the wrong places, and do all the wrong things to find that indescribably happiness that we know we should enjoy!

Every aspect of the world's system: governments, educational systems, medical community, cults, occult and yes the church all promise us a better life. Sadly, however, none of these including many churches offer what God is offering: entrance into the Kingdom of God! Many churches offer a quasi-version of living by faith as the means to a good life. But it is seldom faith in the character and nature of God; it is usually operating faith based on individual needs. By the concept of the Kingdom of God and of Heaven, i.e., entering into a realm whereby we access God's resources because we are in intimate relationship with Him, is seldom presented.

Today education, governments and "science" offer us the false hope of a Utopian society that will finally give man the perfect life. Most of the philosophies upon which these promises are being made have been present in the earth and utilized for decades or even centuries. They have never worked, they never will work, yet the masses place their hope in these "clouds without rain." Why does mankind keep falling for the same deceptive promise of Utopia? It is wired into our DNA. We were created in the likeness and image of God; it is unique to the nature of the human race to know we should experience heaven on earth!

Because of unbelief, we are ready to embrace Luciferian Utopianism as long as it is given an acceptable name: socialism, science, or some other political agenda. Yet the very mention that God has a way we can live in righteousness, peace, and joy, have our emotional, relational and other needs met is rejected as religious fanaticism.

Because the human race is the only species possessing the desire and capability to improve the quality of life by our choices, we will always seek to find ways to make our lives better. The lie of the World's system is the idea that there can be peace among men produced by other men through regulations and philosophies. God, on the other hand, promises there can be peace between you and Him, resulting in peace and joy in your heart, regardless of what is happening in the world around you.[1]

Jesus never offered absolute peace between men until New Jerusalem comes to earth. He never implied any form of government could solve the world's problems or bring peace on earth. He offered a Kingdom we enter into through the doorway in our hearts. He offered us the opportunity to live in the Kingdom realm, based on His finished work combined with our individual trust (faith).

---

1   Luke 17:20-21, The kingdom of God does not come with observation; 21 nor will they say, 'See here!' or 'See there!' For indeed, the Kingdom of God is within you. NKJV

He offered one way to live in the joy and pleasure man had, in the garden, before the fall: the Kingdom of God within!

HeartWork

Read This Aloud Before Every HeartWork Session: The Kingdom of God is internal. HeartWork is designed to remove any internal obstacles that prevent me from entering the realm where I experience Heaven on Earth!

1. Do you believe you were created to live in pleasure and free from pain?

2. Upon what do you base your belief?

3. Do you recognize the deep desire to always improve your life?

4. When you begin to desire a better quality of life, do you go to the Scripture first to determine what God has promised?

5. Do you struggle with guilt, which has been imposed on you by religion, when you desire to have a better life?

6. Do you find yourself looking to politicians, science or other external sources to solve the problems of society?

CHAPTER 15

It's All in Your Mind

What you think today will become your beliefs, your beliefs will become your reality!

As previously established: God desires, and has provided for man to live an incredible life! He is good and only good. He sent Jesus to deliver us from what we deserve while providing for us that which is so much better than what we do deserve: delivered from the curse, qualified for the inheritance and all the promises ours!

In direct opposition to this religious concept of God, is the Garden of Eden. Out of His love for mankind, God created us to live in pleasure, evidenced by the fact that His will was perfectly expressed in His desire for man to live in paradise. When God created the garden, it was free from sickness, pain, and lack. In His desire to protect us, God made our nervous system to detect pain and pleasure. When confronted with even the threat of pain, our fight or flight response is activated to deliver us from the threat of pain. God never intended that we tolerate pain. The garden was the only time and place we can see God's desire for the human race perfectly expressed. If we want to understand God's will for us, we must start by looking at life in the Garden!

Fortunately, God's desire for man is still the same today as it was in the Garden. As contradictory as it may seem to the religious mindset, it was man's choice to decide good and evil for himself that led him to leave paradise to be his own god. It was the inception of *Luciferian doctrine* in the Garden that influenced and proliferated the "angry God" doctrine, throughout the ages. This destructive philosophy teaches that Lucifer is the true savior of men. After all, according to

Luciferian doctrine, he gave us knowledge, which set us free from the moral; and ethical control of the angry Creator God.

Portraying God as harsh and vengeful is based on a twisted concept of sovereignty. Sovereignty denies the second cornerstone of faith: we are created in the likeness and image of God, therefore, we have free will. God never, for any reason violates man's freedom of choice, even if that choice is destructive. God has given us the Truth in His Word. He has poured out His Spirit who speaks to our hearts. Anyone desiring to know the loving character and nature of God can do so!

The false sovereignty message says God can do anything, including violating your will. It also goes on to say, God causes everything that occurs on planet earth. Luciferians say, "since God is in control of the earth, it is easy to see how cruel He is. If He was good, He would make everything come out good." Sadly this Luciferian doctrine is at the core of almost all modern doctrine. It is reinforced every time a loved one dies, and someone says, "we don't know why He took her." God doesn't take people. He is not a murder.

With control as the fulcrum of their propaganda, Luciferians, and many Christians denounce God as a loving Father; after all, if He actually loved us, He would not allow these horrors to occur! Even though all the promises outlined in the Bible corroborate God's intentions toward us, they further claim God seeks to oppress mankind through His *commandments* which serve only to prevent us from the fulfillment of our desires. Sadly, these beliefs are embedded in nearly all factions of modern Christianity. Thus, the doctrine of suffering to become righteous and holy seems to be the undercurrent of much modern theology.

Luciferian doctrine is the ultimate deception rooted in every human philosophy, every cult, and every corrupt governmental policy. Mercifully, the deception is simple, and its cure is even simpler! The deception: by choosing to heed the twisted logic of Satan, man chose to act independently of God's Word and wisdom. With the authority God gave him (Gen. 1:26), man brought every problem that exists on planet earth through our corrupt knowledge. Rather than admit the state of the world is the product of man's will, we blame God under the auspices of sovereignty and control!

Tragically, the Luciferian message of fear and wrath has doomed billions to an eternity apart from God; billions more cling to a God they do not fully trust while awaiting the promise of a better life-after-death (heaven) but never entering the Kingdom of Heaven here on earth. Not only does this distorted concept of God make it impossible to trust Him, but we blame Him for every pain we endure. Hence, God becomes the pain we avoid, and self-gratification becomes the pleasure we pursue. If we are in fact wired to be drawn to pleasure and avoid pain, God is on no one's list for a better life.

Throughout His ministry, Jesus refuted this pervasive, corrupt perception of God by preaching the gospel of the Kingdom of God. The Hebrew mind understood and immediately connected this Kingdom to the Garden: the realm where man enjoys the benefits and resources available to him to the degree he yields his view and opinion to God, i.e., His Lordship. As in every Kingdom, there are two very specific aspects: a king and a realm, wherein the Kingdom of God points us to the rule of the King, while the Kingdom of Heaven points us to the resources of heaven. The only requirement for man to enjoy all God has is faith (trust)!

Our western culture, misunderstands biblical faith, because of what we have been taught for the last 50 years. Simply put, faith does not get God to do things for us. Faith is trust, an essential factor in any relationship. Faith in God is trust for who He has revealed Himself to be, most specifically through the life, teaching, death, burial, and resurrection of Jesus. Among the many reasons faith is so pleasing to God, it is the only way He can know who He is and have a relationship with His children!

In the Old Covenant, a *type* from which we understand all New Covenant truth, the Hebrews brought their sacrifices to God. The Hebrew word for *sacrifice* means *to come close or draw near*. Contrary to what we have been told, the Old Covenant was not fear-based to appease an angry God nor was it works-based to earn our righteousness or His blessings. The *roll call of faith* in Hebrews 11 makes it very clear that faith, or trust, is the only way anyone has ever pleased God.

The Old Covenant sacrifices had to be done in faith. *"Faith for what?"* we might ask. Rather than trying to earn right-standing with God, the sacrifices were designed to influence man's heart as he sought to reconnect to God. According to Allen Ross in his wonderful book, *Holiness to the Lord*, before giving an offering, the people were examined by the priest to determine if they were actually in faith, or trusting what God had promised.

Only when faith was present could a sacrifice have a positive influence on the heart of the giver. The Holy God of Israel being unique and uncommon, unlike all the pagan gods of the world, did not need sacrifices as a bribe. The worshippers of Jehovah did not sacrifice for God's benefit; they sacrificed for their own. On some level, every offering was an appeal to *draw near* (Korban) to God. Whether dealing with a known sin or just the desire to experience a connection to God, the concept was simple: God promised to always be near and to always accept their *draw near* offerings. Therefore, we can trust He is loving and kind; therefore the separation between us and Him lies within our hearts, not His. So, when we draw near to Him, He is already there attempting to draw near to us! This is repeated in Heb. 13:5, *"I will never leave you nor forsake you."*

When the Hebrews made offerings, they selected a specific offering that most closely related to their sin or offense, i.e., the action that had negatively affected their hearts. Many times they offered what was the most anticipated of all [personal offerings]: the peace offering. The peace offering was cause for celebration because the source of separation (guilt in their heart) had been removed, they were reconciled to God, not by the offering, but by faith in the offering.

From the Hebrew perspective, peace meant health, healing, prosperity, protection, deliverance and almost every positive aspect of a full life was available. The peace offering was a joyous declaration of their hearts that said, *I am intimately connected to God; therefore, all His resources are available to me!*

Through this process of reconnecting to God, peace with God was experienced, with all its implication of provision that resulted in a tranquil state of mind. Having entered into peace they felt a sense of righteousness—life was once again *as it should be.* This was immediately followed by a celebration during which they shared their peace offering with all who were present. They testified to their own foolishness and God's enduring mercy. It was a joyful occasion; hence, the Kingdom of God is righteousness, peace, and joy.

Unlike present-day believers, the Hebrew worshipper had no illusion of access to the resources of God apart from an intimate relationship with Him. In fact, God rebuked them more than once for their hypocrisy. They didn't want God they wanted what they could get from Him. They sought the benefits to give them quality of life. We all know, however, quality of life has never been found in possessions, but rather, in the relationships we experience. The people of faith brought their offering because they wanted to reconnect to God personally.

In the Hebrew language, all the letters are also numbers. God created all that exists in mathematical equations; therefore, it only stands to reason that His language of choice would be as numerical as it is intellectual. In Hebrew, numbers can convey meanings just as surely as words. When words or phrases have identical numeric values, this indicates a connection. This is called Gematria, not to be confused with numerology.

The words *heaven* and *mind* have an identical numeric value; therefore, people understood from the beginning, and even more clearly after listening to Jesus' teaching, the way we think and believe is essential for entering the Kingdom realm. When Jesus stated that the Kingdom did not come by outward observation but was found within, He was not saying anything new. The problem was, however, the religious rulers were not interested in a Kingdom that was within, one that required repentance and transformation. They were not much different than their Roman counterparts. Lust for power drove their desire for a Kingdom that would give the Jewish nation rule of the world, not a moral Kingdom that ruled in our hearts!

Jesus said this when seeking to find *zoe,* the quality of life possessed by God, *"Enter by the narrow gate; for wide is the gate and broad is the way that leads to de-*

struction, and there are many who go in by it. Because narrow is the gate and difficult is the way which leads to life, and there are few who find it." (Matt. 7:13-14) The reason we do not experience the quality of life offered by Kingdom living is simply the refusal to surrender our view and opinion to God. We would rather be right than whole. The narrow gate is depicted on the Hebrew letter Hei, which has a narrow gap at the top. The wide gate of destruction is the way of the world.

Jesus' message of the Kingdom is this: inside you is a realm wherein you can enter now to experience a deep personal connection with God and all the resources of heaven. The only requirements for entry are trust in God and surrender to His rule (Lordship). The born-again experience is free and open to all, but the path of life must be chosen by the believer. Believers who trust Jesus' representation of God and His interpretation of Scripture, rather than mainstream theology, renew their minds to harmonize with the life He modeled, His teachings, and His death, burial, and resurrection. Then, with complete faith, they confidently open their hearts to see, perceive, understand and enjoy that which was previously hidden to them by their fear and unbelief. Believers live life in the invisible Kingdom of the heart, inwardly experiencing all that God is and all that God has.

The thoughts of the mind are the doorkeeper of the heart. What we think about ultimately determines what gets into our heart. Our thoughts are the measure we meet, concerning the Word of God we hear. According to Jesus, this is the one factor determining the quantity and quality of life that we derive from the Word we hear. When we renew our mind to create an awareness of the promises and provision of God through the Lord Jesus, that eventually becomes the beliefs of our heart. If you notice and celebrate all the good things of God, you will have heaven in your mind. Eventually, you will have heaven in your heart. When the heart, mind agree you create and experience a new reality.

HeartWork

Read This Aloud Before Every HeartWork Session: The Kingdom of God is internal. HeartWork is designed to remove any internal obstacles that prevent me from entering the realm where I experience Heaven on Earth!

1. Will you spend the next 30 days memorizing at least 100 promises of God that are yours in Jesus?

2. If so, will you put forth an effort to recognize the things in your life that are working as God promised and begin to give thanks and celebrate them?

3. Will you notice the parts of your life that are incongruent with the promises, and when you notice those things will you quote a promise of God and speak to the situation insisting that it align with the promise?

CHAPTER 16

Facing My Ultimate Fear

You can die once and be resurrected, or die the death of a thousand cuts

One of Jesus most ignored warning may be that we, *"make the word of God of no effect through your tradition."* (Mark 7:13) The religious mind would quickly declare, nothing can make the Word of God void of power. But the writer of Hebrews would disagree, *"... the word which they heard did not profit them, not being mixed with faith in those who heard it."* (Heb 4:2) Likewise the Psalmist points out, *"...again and again, they tempted God, And limited the Holy One of Israel."* (Ps 78:41) Tradition and culture is the plague of the 21st-century church.

God Word is like unto seed. It must be planted in the soil. The soil must first be tilled. When the soil receives the seed. It must then be watered and fertilized. The final influence on the growth of the seed is, thorns must not only be removed, but they must not be planted among the good seed, otherwise it will choke out the seed before it can produce a harvest! The Bible and very specifically Jesus' teaching.

Entering into and living in the realm of the Kingdom is all about faith, not faith for things; faith in God. Do we believe God is who He proclaimed Himself to be, through His names, the Scripture, the life and teachings of Jesus, but most specifically, through what He accomplished in His death, burial and resurrection? For over half a century there has been a predominance of teaching about "faith for things." The tragedy is people don't seem to have for life. It's what I call "walking around faith." This is the faith that believes and receives the grace to live a godly life, provide for our family, walk in love and be as we should be in Jesus!

To a large degree, we are the product of our environment, culture, and education. To a large degree, our sense of right and wrong has nothing to do with what the Bible says. There are some who determine right and wrong very subjectively. If the behavior gets them what they want, or makes them feel good, it is judged as good. Then there are those who believe if it is legal according to civil law it's good. Since 1970 one report says there have been over 44 million abortions. Many Christians believe abortions are moral because they are legal and the medical community supports them. Somehow they forget that all the same political experts considered lynching a black man was legal and moral less than a century ago.

The Word of God gives several warnings about how culture and community can help us or destroy us. 1 Cor 15:33, in the NIV, sums it up best, *"Do not be misled: "Bad company corrupts good character."* The Bible is full of warnings against "hanging out" spending time with, and taking on the traits of the ungodly. If we are more open to, and more capable of hearing the voices of other people, those people will influence our lives more than God Himself!

Even those seeking to walk with God are usually unaware of how little they believe the Bible and how much they are influenced by religious traditions that neutralize the world of God. Our culture and tradition shape the way we see the world and ourselves. Therefore, they become the basis for interpreting God's Word. Unwittingly we reject Jesus rules of interpretation: *"'You shall love the Lord your God with all your heart, with all your soul, and with all your mind.' This is the first and great commandment. 39 And the second is like it: 'You shall love your neighbor as yourself.' On these two commandments hang all the Law and the Prophets."* (Matt. 22:37-40) But Jesus didn't leave us with the rules, He then modeled exactly what it would look like when put into practice.

But the greatest dearth of the Word of God is the refusal of Christians to prayerfully read the Bible for themselves. They choose rather to have others become the mediator between them and God. Rather than search Jesus' teachings, pray for direction and trust God to be a true Father, they want others to read the Word for them. They reject Jesus' interpretations and application and replace them with those of their leaders. Sadly, very little of the Word of God is taught in many pulpits; therefore people are attempting to operate faith on someone's personal or denominational interpretation, never knowing the Word of God or the God of the Word for themselves.

No one can believe a truth they haven't heard or read; no one will believe a truth that opposes their culture if they are not repentant and teachable, and no one will surrender what they have trusted unless they trust the source of the new information. That which defies personal life experience will nearly always be rejected as a lie. The lie heard repeatedly will be believed before the truth can be validated; thus, the saying, *he who has, gets more of what he already has.* Emerging as overcomers from the trap of unbelief, with so many Influences working against us, depends almost entirely on two factors: the condition of our hearts and the version of the gospel we hear.

Our personal reality is not what we see; it is what we perceive. How we perceive and understand anything is influenced by life experience, previous teaching, and the resulting judgments which arise based on these influences. On one occasion, when an expert in the law asked Jesus what he must do to inherit eternal life, Jesus answered the question with a question, *"What is written in the Law, and how do you read it?"* (Luke 10:26, NIV) His point was that it is not simply a matter of reading the Bible, it is what we read *into* the Bible that determines our beliefs.

Jesus was not being coy when He asked this question, but rather with the intention of revealing the man's predetermined beliefs. God always attempts to bring us to the light, for it is never His will that we remain in darkness. The truth that will open our eyes is always the truth to which we have closed our eyes and hardened our heart. That's why the truth with the most potential to set one free always has the most potential to offend.

Jesus understood tradition is always influencing our perceptions and biblical interpretations based on the life influences, education, and social constructs we have accepted as the standard for normal. The *unrepentant* (*opposer of truth*) interprets the Bible based on predetermined, traditional views, while the repentant disciple interprets personal views based on the Word of God, i.e., what Jesus modeled and taught.

How most Christians read and interpret the Bible in no way ensures their understanding is harmonious with God's intended interpretation or application. Those who fervently apply their own interpretations with all sincerity but continue to experience their lives getting worse will most likely blame God or, while still clinging to Him, despise Him in their hearts.

As humans, we do not like the unknown. Functioning in our idea of the known gives us a false sense of control and security. Even those who enjoy change may alter their activities or other superficial endeavors but rarely change their beliefs. Beliefs are the filters through which we view the world, shape our perception, and determine good and evil (danger, threat, hardship). What we perceive creates an interpretation of the world which we call a *paradigm*. We all have a personal *paradigm: a distinct set of concepts or thought patterns by which we determine reality.*

Our life experience is like a closed loop. We are raised in and influenced by a culture that embraces a particular worldview, shaping the way we see and interpret reality. Our worldview, then, becomes an interpretation of reality based largely on the sum total of our judgments. Therefore, our interaction with the world affects us not based on reality, but on our perception of reality. The subsequent emotions and experiences invoked by our predefined reality determine our actions. Our actions, in turn, provoke the reactions of others, and a destructive cyclical process ensues that continuously affirms our false interpretation of reality.

Surrendering the beliefs that create a false sense of reality is the emotional equivalent of dying (to self), forsaking the world we know, and entering into a realm that is completely unknown. When entering into the Kingdom, this realm is only unknown if we do not believe the teaching of Jesus, and the other writers of the New Testament. When we become one with Christ, through faith in His death, burial, and resurrection, we have a sense of "knowing" that goes beyond our actual life experience.

Dying to self involves surrendering our opinions, assumptions, and judgments to God. Entering the Kingdom, however, occurs when we choose to believe and govern our lives by the Word of God as taught, interpreted and modeled by Jesus. Until we surrender our lives to Him as Lord, we cannot enter His Kingdom. Otherwise, we become like the children of Israel who crossed the Red Sea with Moses but refused to trust God enough to enter the Promised Land, leaving us born again but wandering pointlessly in the wilderness.

The writer of Hebrews points out that the fear of death keeps us bound to the devil.

> *Inasmuch then as the children have partaken of flesh and blood, He Himself likewise shared in the same, that through death He might destroy him who had the power of death, that is, the devil, and release those who through fear of death were all their lifetime subject to bondage,* Heb. 2:14-15.

There are a few things we should point out about this scripture. First, this is referring to what Jesus by becoming a man and conquering the devil as a man. On the cross, He settled the sin issue once and for all. Now, all who trust His finished work can enjoy freedom from the power of sin.

It says through His death He destroyed the power of the devil. The word destroy in the original language means, to be (render) entirely idle (useless);[1] or, "to condemn to inactivity," "to destroy," and "to take out of the sphere of activity." Keep in mind, the devil didn't have any real or legitimate authority or power over man, his power was through man's fear of death.

This reference to the fear of death may well be more than mere physical death. The Greek word for death can be literal, figurative, physical, spiritual or emotional. After the fall, man ceased to be a living soul and alive to God. The soul is that part of our being where we experience things emotionally. Man's soul was no longer infused with the Life of God producing satisfaction, peace, and joy. He was now flesh; therefore he would now seek to have those feelings and emotions

---

1   Biblesoft's New Exhaustive Strong's Numbers and Concordance with Expanded Greek-Hebrew Dictionary. Copyright © 1994, 2003, 2006 Biblesoft, Inc. and International Bible Translators, Inc.

by gratifying the natural senses of the flesh: taste, touch, hearing, seeing, smelling and the pride of life.

Today, because of Jesus' finished work, we now have a choice: we can live yielded to the Spirit, or we can live yielded to the flesh. The person of faith realizes, yielding to the righteousness of God, empowered by the Holy Spirit produces righteousness, peace, and joy in our soul. The believer knows, no gratification of the flesh is comparable to this. The carnal, i.e., natural minded believer, seeks inner satisfaction through fulfilling the desires of the flesh.

The book of Romans addresses the issue of carnal Christianity. This book is written to Christians not the unsaved. It exposes the deception: sin has no consequences for the believer. But Paul, and the entire Bible say just the opposite.

> *For those who live according to the flesh set their minds on the things of the flesh, but those who live according to the Spirit, the things of the Spirit. For to be carnally minded is death, but to be spiritually minded is life and peace. Because the carnal mind is enmity against God; for it is not subject to the law of God, nor indeed can be. So then, those who are in the flesh cannot please God,* Rom 8:5-8.

For the carnal minded, death isn't merely the end of physical life; death is the end of a life fulfilled by selfish, flesh gratifying desires. When any sense of a fulfilled life resulting from the gratification of the flesh, is taken away from us, it is experienced as a form of death.

This is why the carnal (natural) minded person is so opposed to the commandments. They see the commandments, which are simply teaching us how to walk in love, as something that takes away their personal happiness and gratification.

The core lie of Luciferianism is this: The Creator God is not good, He seeks to keep the human race from the pleasures of the five senses. His commandments serve only to keep mankind from the ultimate pleasures. Lucifer brought knowledge (light) and set mankind free from the Creator. By rejecting God and His commandments, we can fulfill our every desire (lust) with no guilt or shame.

I once heard Anton Lavey say, the truest form of satanism is not worshipping the devil, it is selfishness. Living in the flesh is when we put self-gratification, ahead of walking in love. It is the line in the sand between walking in righteousness and sin, spiritually minded verses carnal minded, and living in the Kingdom versus living in the world system.

The person who dies to self, i.e., recognizes when they are acting from selfishness and makes the appropriate correction, wins over the fear of physical death. They begin to participate in the resurrected life of Jesus now! Therefore they have no fear of death, emotional or physical. They are already living in newness of life!

HeartWork

Read This Aloud Before Every HeartWork Session: The Kingdom of God is internal. HeartWork is designed to remove any internal obstacles that prevent me from entering the realm where I experience Heaven on Earth!

1. Do I identify as a Baptist, Methodist, charismatic, etc., more than seeing myself as a child of God?

2. Do I really believe sin destroys my changes at a great life?

3. Have I deliberately chosen to walk in love toward others?

4. On a scale of 1-10, 1 being the lowest what percentages of decisions do I make, putting other people needs ahead of my own?

5. Do I see the commandments as God's prescription for walking in love or as rules?

CHAPTER 17

Opening the Eyes of Our Heart

We are all blind to that which contradicts our life experience!

In the first public address of his ministry, Jesus proclaimed that His primary objective was to heal our broken hearts (Luke 4:18). Until our hearts are healed, we cannot function consistently in faith. Our beliefs are corrupted, and our capacity for a life of righteousness, peace, and joy is nonexistent. Several factors are necessary for experiencing healing in our hearts, but it starts with preaching the gospel of the Kingdom to the poor; those who lack what they need to be whole.

We are all in some form or fashion struggling with our past: our childhood, and cellular memories, i.e., that which has been done to us, that which we have witnessed, and that which we have done to others. All of those factors come together to influence our heart, thus affecting our heart's capacity for some of life's most essential functions. Faith, love, self-worth, fear, every other core value and belief that directs our life is a matter of the heart.

A broken or wounded heart suffers from the fear that what happened in the past will occur again; therefore, trust becomes subservient to our fearful expectations of the future, based on wounds of the past. A person who has not had faithfulness modeled to them has difficulty trusting. All pain of the past, manifesting in irrational emotions or behavior in the present is a form of PTSD.

Healing the broken heart is the beginning of an internal journey that leads to emotional health, and ultimately to the Kingdom of God. The parables of the Kingdom are only understood when belief in the heart is the core factor of interpretation. As freewill beings, created in God's own image, every step along the path to a better life than we have known must be a choice based on our trust for God and what He accomplished through the Lord Jesus Christ. Before a choice can be made, we must first be able to "see," and the light of God's reality must shine into our darkness making the choices visible.

When Jesus referred to *"the poor in spirit, for theirs is the kingdom of heaven"* (Matt. 5:3), the word *poor* is not a reference to the financially poor. The word *poor* literally means t*o be crouched down with an extended hand like a beggar.* The *poor in spirit* understand their destitution and captivity to spiritual poverty. The outstretched hand represents the realization of the need, plus desire and willing-ness to receive. For that reason, the Kingdom of Heaven, used in reference to poor beggars, points us to the resources of provision and protection always avail-able in the Kingdom of God.

Jesus' authoritative proclamation, in Luke 4:18, declares freedom from the cap-tivity that keeps us bound in the destitution of our worldly paradigm. The word *captives* in this verse represents not only those who do not have what they need to be set free, but the fact that they are prisoners of war, captured by their arch enemy (fear and unbelief) through the deceitfulness of sin. Sin is always rooted in the illusion of lack, i.e., not being enough, or qualified for the life we desire. The lack in a person's life may be real, but it is an illusion when we consider that God's resources are always available to those who trust Him.

Recovering sight to the blind appears to be the pivotal point in the succession leading to a healed heart, freedom, and access to the resources of heaven. The New Testament word for *"blind"* does not always mean physical blindness; it can also refer to an impairment, dim, partial, or distorted perception. Jesus Himself is the light of the world. When we believe the truth about Him, we have the light making it possible to see from God's perspective. Jesus wants us to see the way clear to the Father and His resources.

Jesus came to make the crooked path straight, plain, and safe to walk. He is the way, so we know where we're going. He is our Shepherd to protect and prevent us from being frightened or lost along the way. Ironically, the path to safety that is obvious to some may look dark and foreboding to others who do not have the light. But Jesus is only these things to those who believe on His resurrection and surrender to Him as Lord.

Jesus preached, the gospel of the Kingdom has the power to heal and set free those who are crushed, broken, and bruised, but only for those who are will-ing to hear and yield to the truth they hear (repent). It is generally agreed when proclaiming His purpose in Luke 4, Jesus was quoting Isaiah 58:6, *"Is this not the fast that I have chosen: To loose the bonds of wickedness, To undo the heavy burdens, To let the oppressed go free, And that you break every yoke?"* The *bonds of wickedness*

95

represent anything that puts us in pain, distress, hardship, or suffering.

Isaiah actually completes this passage by preceding it with a reference to the Year of Jubilee (v. 5), when he says He (Jesus) will *"proclaim the acceptable year of the Lord."* Every 50 years the Hebrews were to celebrate the year of Jubilee, a time when all debts were paid. It did not matter if the debt had been incurred responsibly or irresponsibly; every debt was paid and the inheritance restored to those in debt. This undeserved freedom was based on the love, faithfulness, and goodness of God. From this, we can clearly see God's goodness is intended to bring us to repentance. Until we repent (change our minds) about the beliefs and behaviors that have taken us captive, we will never escape captivity. The message the *poor in spirit* hear must be the Gospel (Good News) of the Kingdom, which expresses how God's goodness released us from our captivity, and we now have a choice to live in that freedom or remain in captivity.

This messianic prophecy has always intrigued me in relation to opening blind eyes.

> *I, the Lord, have called You in righteousness, And will hold Your hand; I will keep You and give You as a covenant to the people, As a light to the Gentiles, To open blind eyes, To bring out prisoners from the prison, Those who sit in darkness from the prison house* (Isa. 42:6-7).

The *prisoners* he refers to are those who remain captive to the darkness of their beliefs and cannot see that the prison door has been opened. Their *blindness* is the consequence of their beliefs. To see, they must open their eyes to the choice they have, to believe or reject the truth.

In our home, we have a room that is the *safe zone* for our cats. I conditioned my dog to never go into that room. I established an invisible boundary he was not allowed to cross. Through conditioning, that version of reality was programmed into his brain by repetition, reward, and response. Now, when he walks up to the doorway, he stops to wait for my permission to cross that invisible line. Because we have been conditioned by the imaginary prison door of our beliefs, we remain *stuck* in darkness. These beliefs hold us in poverty, sickness, unhappiness and a life of continual lack! We need only to realize that the door only exists in our heart. It is not locked, we can believe the truth about Jesus, see the situation for what it is and choose to walk out.

When Jesus fed the five thousand, He had the opportunity to doubt God's power in Him. If I had a few fish and loaves of bread and needed to feed thousands, I know what my temptation would be: doubt. I would fear that I did not have the faith and that I would make a fool of myself in front of the people. So, if Jesus was tempted like us in every way, that would also be His temptation.

Mark 6:41 says, *"And when He had taken the five loaves and the two fish, He looked up to heaven, blessed, and broke the loaves."* Before attempting to operate in faith, Jesus modeled exactly what we should do when we find ourselves in fear and doubt: *He looked to heaven.* The original language reveals that He did more than just look up in the sky. This phrase has the same root word as the one in Luke 4:18 *opening blind eyes.* Opening the eyes of the blind is not about physical blindness; it is about the beliefs that blind us. It is this blindness that keeps us from perceiving not only to our freedom but our access to the Kingdom of Heaven: the reality of God's limitless resources. Jesus looked to the Kingdom of Heaven, connected with the Father, and *recovered His sight.*

Do we see our circumstances from God's perspective of limitless possibilities or from the perspective determined by our life experiences? When our life paradigm is being shaped by life experiences rather than God's reality, our circumstances cause us to perceive and ultimately believe that we are limited to our own abilities, resources, health, family, race, environment, etc. Fixating on circumstances to determine our course of action instead of looking to the promises we have in Christ, blinds us to all God's resources, leaving us *stuck* in our distorted reality: lack with no provision!

When we perceive and choose to believe what God has accomplished in Christ, we realize the metaphorical prison door of our circumstances has already been opened, and all we must do is make the choice to trust God, to walk out of our prison of unbelief and into the limitless possibilities of His kingdom. Since we are not imprisoned by Satan, there are no demons to fight. All we must believe for the door to open is what Jesus already accomplished through His death, burial and resurrection. When we hear and believe the truth, we enter into faith (trust) which is in itself an act of repentance. Repentance need not be an emotionally defined, individual step in the process, but rather the natural progression from recognizing our unbelief to choosing to believe the truth. Changing our mind becomes an organic process.

The Apostle Paul said in Romans 10:17: *"Faith comes by hearing and hearing by the Word of God."* In Greek, *Word* refers to the topic or specific utterance of the one preaching the message. We tend to lift this verse out of context and translate it as *repeatedly hearing the Scripture,* but a hard, crooked, or darkened heart will not interpret the Scripture consistent with God's intention. Hearing the same Scripture over and over, apart from repentance, only reinforces the corrupt interpretation that holds us in bondage.

To grasp the context of faith in its entirety, we must look back at verse 15 to realize that what we hear proclaimed must be the Gospel of Peace, if we are to have true biblical faith. The Gospel of Peace is the good news of the Covenant of Peace God made with Jesus who obtained all the inheritance: the resources of the Kingdom of Heaven, available to us now.

When we believe on His resurrection from our hearts and confess Him as Lord, we can share in His inheritance. Everything we are delivered from (wrath, judgment, and death) and all the promises we are given is received by His faith at the resurrection. Jesus paid the price we should pay, freeing us from that debt. He died the death we should die; therefore we are free from death. He defeated the devil so we don't have to fight that battle. He won the victory and we share in that victory. He rose from the dead giving us resurrection life. He obtained an inheritance which He shares with us. God made the covenant with Jesus, so we do not have to earn the inheritance.

Our responsibility is to persuade our hearts of what Jesus accomplished and what we have in Him, until our hearts are fully convinced (immovable faith) of what Jesus accomplished through His death, burial, and resurrection. When we believe this Gospel of peace, faith opens our eyes and our hearts to see. Because we trust Him we follow Him through the narrow gate of godliness and faith into the Kingdom where we live in the inheritance!

This is the Good News message of the cross! Whether unbelievers coming to Jesus for the first time or believers facing the challenges of life, experiencing all that we are and all that is rightfully ours (our inheritance) in Him is based solely on our faith in the resurrection of Christ. The Good News of the Gospel of Peace is the message of light that reveals God's love, opening our eyes in the midst of our darkness, enabling us to walk out the open door!

HeartWork

Read This Aloud Before Every HeartWork Session: The Kingdom of God is internal. HeartWork is designed to remove any internal obstacles that prevent me from entering the realm where I experience Heaven on Earth!

The following question will provide you with an exercise that could last for months or even a lifetime. One of the main ways we realize if we believe the truth is how we live it with others. After answering this question I will suggest a few exercises that will allow you to reach an honest answer.

1. Do I have a repentant attitude?

2. Will I accept that my feeling of lack is an illusion caused by my beliefs?

3. Will I prayerfully read the New Testament, listening in my heart to find the truths which will open my eyes?

CHAPTER 18

My Version of Paradise

For the selfish to live in paradise, the rest of the world has to live in hell!

In every facet of life, it seems we only have two choices, life or death, blessings or cursing, being the head or the tail, being above or not beneath, being the lender or the borrower and etc. Everything, every decision is leading us in one direction or the other, there is no middle ground. One is the way of the World the other is the Kingdom of God!

God has made a way for us to always have the very best life has to offer, That way of life is defined by God. It comes to us in the form of promises. If we trust God and His promises we find ourselves in the Kingdom of God: righteousness, peace, and joy in the Holy Spirit. If not, we find ourselves in the flesh (wilderness). 2 Peter 1:3-4 tells us:

His divine power has given to us all things that pertain to life and godliness, through the (experiential) knowledge of Him who called us by glory and virtue, by which have been given to us exceedingly great and precious promises, that through these you may be partakers of the divine nature, having escaped the corruption that is in the world through lust.

There is no path to the kingdom other than trusting and following God. He is attempting to lead us to something we have never seen, a place we've never been that is astronomically better than anything we've ever experienced. However, not everyone is willing to trust God to that extent, and some just do not want God's version of the good life.

The greatest commandment to Israel is: *"Hear, O Israel: The Lord our God, the Lord is one! You shall love the Lord your God with all your heart, with all your soul, and with all your strength, And these words which I command you today shall be in your heart."* (Deut. 6:4-7)

We know the high regard held for this verse because of Hebrew history and the traditions related to the reciting of this commandment. However, Jesus shows us the true understanding and application of this verse, He said it was the most important of all commandments. Jesus, however, put the application of this commandment into practice when He quoted Leviticus 19:18, *And you shall love your neighbor as yourself.*

By adding the second commandment, the first was put into a context, which gave us a way to qualify the application of the first!. Jesus even went further to explain, *On these two commandments hang all the Law and the Prophets* (Matt. 22:40). From the moment they were uttered, the commandments were actually prescriptions for how to express love to others as God Himself expresses it. As has been said by the sages, *God's words are not legalistic rules—His words are prescriptions* for how to be holy like God is holy, and how to walk in love.

Loving God could be twisted into every extreme form of legalism imaginable without context, and that is exactly what the Jews did. Because the Jews didn't understand God's love for man, they were able to heap all manner of burdens on the people in the name of, "If you love God you'll obey." The commandments instead of showing us how to treat one another fairly became the basis for judging others. What the believer should have internalized to apply to their own life became the microscope under which they scrutinized others.

The ruling religious body attempted to do what God Himself would not do: force mankind to love Him. Even worse, the religious basis for love had nothing to do with heart belief. When Jesus quoted from Leviticus, it became clear that total love for God, experienced and expressed from every aspect of our being, was the same love we must have for our fellow man. We cannot, therefore, take God's prescription for loving Him to be interpreted and applied in any way that violates love toward our neighbor, ignoring the fact that it must come from our heart.

In the prescription to *love our neighbor as ourselves*, we encounter one of the most important foundational truths in all of Jesus' teaching. It provides the most significant understanding of God's will and original intention for mankind, opening the door to theological interpretation concerning all matters. It is the cornerstone of New Covenant theology, as it should have been for the Old Covenant. It is the supreme guide to understanding everything God has ever said or done, and it defines the New Covenant believers' connection to the Old Testament commandments. It identifies the narrow path that leads to Kingdom life, and more than any Word ever uttered by God, it determines whether we are surrendered to the Lordship of Jesus or passive workers of iniquity.

The nation of Israel is a *type*, or example, of the believer in pursuit of the Kingdom of God. Canaan was a place promised to the Children of Israel which could only be entered by trusting and following God's prescriptions. The legalistic heart interprets God's prescriptions as a means of earning that which has been promised, but to the one who knows and trusts the love of God, commandments are viewed completely differently. To the faithful of heart, commandments are not misconstrued as rules by which we earn anything from God, but rather the fatherly wisdom by which God guides us to the treasures of life. If the Israelites had walked in love as God defined it, they would have always enjoyed peace, prosperity, and security. They would have been a light to all the nations of the world, showing the justice of God. Theirs would have been the Kingdom of God, a nation in full compliance with the wisdom of God, making it possible for Him to be their Divine Leader and Protector. Theirs would have been the Kingdom of Heaven, wherein they could experience Divine provision.

The Kingdom of God is where God's loving, wise rule reigns in the heart of man because it is trusted and followed, making it possible for Him to be both Provider and Protector. Nevertheless, with the capacity to interpret good and evil, they sometimes trusted God and sometimes trusted themselves. God offered them the wisdom for a peaceful government, justice for all, protection from their enemies, fertile land, a stable economy, and everything else needed for a life of righteousness, peace, and joy. According to the Apostle Paul, the nation of Israel's history is also a *type* for us to understand the way to live. It clearly demonstrates how sin can set us off course, while simultaneously encouraging the repentance that can get us back on course as we journey toward our inheritance: the kingdom of God!

The writer of Hebrews addresses believers who have not entered into rest. We often assume this conversation to be directed to the lost and the *rest* to be a reference to the born-again experience, but that is absolutely not the case. The Israelites were given a promise of entering into a land that would be theirs, but only by following God's wisdom. Why is it so important that we trust and obey God, you might ask? The nations that inhabited Canaan were wicked haters of God. They were types of our flesh. We cannot defeat them, in our own power. We need God to provide the strategy and the power for us to live victoriously in our inheritance.

The Apostle Paul parallels the Israelites exodus from Egypt with the believer abandoning the control of this world's system. Delivered from slavery, the Israelites represent our freedom from sin. Their participation in the first Passover typifies our deliverance from wrath, judgment, and death by the blood of Christ. The crossing of the Red Sea illustrates our baptism into Christ. His Word and

His wisdom would have led them to their inheritance, but, sadly, it was never allowed to take root in their hearts. Like the hearts described in the parable of the sower, they refused to trust God; consequently, they did not have the power or the wisdom to enter the Promised Land, the Kingdom of God.

Hebrews 3:18-19 shows us what the Israelites could not and would not do as a result of their unbelief. God said, *"And to whom did He swear that they would not enter His rest, but to those who did not obey?"* The legalist would read this and interpret it to mean God would not allow them to enter into this rest as punishment for unbelief. Verse 19, however, explains, because of unbelief, they could not enter in. So, we see that they could not enter in because of unbelief. This was not God's punishment; it was their choice not to trust Him to overcome the inhabitants.

Would people who refused to trust God for daily provision and basic needs be ready to enter the land of Canaan and conquer the enemy, many of whom were giants? No! If God had attempted to take them into a land where they could not trust Him for deliverance, the entire nation would have been destroyed and the bloodline of the Messiah lost. This is not a matter of God predicting what they would do when they arrived in Canaan and thwarting their opportunity. The Israelites had previously reached the shores of the Jordan and had been given the opportunity to enter the land. They simply did not trust God could or would deliver the promise. As Hebrews explains, it was in their unbelief that they put God on trial and declared Him guilty of perjury on His promise. By choosing to wander the wilderness rather than trust God, they got exactly what they chose: a life less than what they could have had.

The person who has found their sense of identity and their fulfillment in life through the natural senses: hearing, seeing, taste, touch, smell and the pride of life are addicted. Giving up the way of life that gives them pleasure is the death to self they are not willing to accept. After all, they have no other life experience. They are no different than any other addict; they will destroy themselves and everyone around them rather than give up their addiction to self-gratification.

Today's culture sees walking love, being merciful and forgiving as being weak. They have no desire for those characteristics. They do not want the Kingdom God is promising. They do not want to walk in love; they do not want to prefer anyone above themselves. Yet, they daily bemoan the pain of the life they have chosen, but it is the life they have chosen, and God will not violate their will.

It is relatively easy to identify this behavior in gangs or extreme groups. But it is, in fact, this same illogical rationale that keeps us from living in the Kingdom today. The person who is able to control their spouse by fear doesn't trust the power of love working in their heart. Rather than give up the need to control and find peace, we would rather hold to that which is giving us what we want.

The Bible tells us to taste and see that the Lord is good. We can never intellectually know how great it is to live in righteousness, peace, and joy until we taste it for ourselves. Every time we have a positive experience walking in God's love we will gain the confidence to branch out into other areas of life. At some point, we will decide to take the plunge and surrender our life.

We can determine ourselves smarter than God, get the version of heaven we create, or we can trust God, our Creator, an inter into a dimension beyond our wildest dreams.

HeartWork

Read This Aloud Before Every HeartWork Session: The Kingdom of God is internal. HeartWork is designed to remove any internal obstacles that prevent me from entering the realm where I experience Heaven on Earth!

1. What are you afraid you'll lose if you stop controlling and begin walking in love?

2. Is your present approach to having the life you desire actually working?

3. Does your present approach give you peace and joy in your heart?

4. Does your present approach allow others to exercise their free will and make choices for themselves, or does it require control and manipulation on your part?

5. Does the Gospel you believe present a positive, life-affirming concept of Kingdom living that is so compelling it provides all you want and all you need?

CHAPTER 19

I Get What I Choose

I may not get what I want, but I always get what I choose!

Our understanding of cause and effect is incredibly distorted when it comes to God, man, authority and free will. Once again, we revisit the parable of the sower in Matthew 13, *"Whoever has will be given more, and he will have an abundance; whoever does not have, even what he has will be taken away from him."* When there is a lack of trust for God and His Word, we are in doubt or unbelief. Doubt can be the struggle between two opinions, or it can mean that we have determined to be unpersuadable. Unbelief gets down to judging God as untrustworthy. However, because of our internal mind game we need to sanitize that definition, so, we create justifications, rather than simply admit we do not consider God faithful to His promise: a liar! Regardless of the particulars of our internal process, unbelief puts the promise beyond our capacity to receive.

Religion has perpetrated the Luciferian doctrine that as *Sovereign*, God can do anything He wants on planet earth. To follow that logic, we must believe God has absolute power and control, which means, when anything bad happens, it is God's will. To support this belief, we must then task ourselves with developing a twisted, circumstantial theology to explain why we are not experiencing the promises of God. The flaws in this twisted logic are unending; the corrupt fruit that grows from this seed is cancerous. But at the end of the process, we will ever accept our responsibility for what is or is not happening in our life.

Understanding the universal laws governing man and God's interaction begins with believing we have a free will because we are created in the likeness and image of God. We must then accept, God cannot give us a free will and then force us to do anything. He leads but does not push, convicts (persuades) but does not force, teaches but does not demand. He provides the prescription, and if we trust Him, we follow. The choice is always ours, and the consequences cannot be separated from the choice.

The law of the seed is the universal law upholding all things in the universe, tangible, emotional or spiritual. The first law of the seed says, "Every seed bears after it's own kind." There is no exception to this law. Every decision we make is a seed that produces fruit in our lives consistent with the seed. The seed isn't just the words spoken, it includes the intention, motive and sometimes even the way we say the words. We have this unscriptural idea that we can treat people any way we desire and God can still make everything work out to our liking. According to Jesus, the law of the seed is the key to understanding everything God has to say about Kingdom living!

On the continuum of man's corrupt logic concerning God's sovereignty, we have the distorted idea that if God loves us, He should keep anything bad from happening to us, but in light of foundational truth, this is just a continuation of more flawed logic. The problem is, we cannot ignore the one absolute truth that God loves us perfectly. 1 John 4:18 tells us that, *Perfect love drives out all fear because fear has to do with punishment.* In other words, perfect love knows God isn't the one punishing us for our choice. Consequences, good or bad, are the fruit of the seed we plant.

Unbelief deceives us into believing we can walk a path other than the one God has prescribed, yet, still experience all He has promised. This is all based on a non-scriptural definition of love. Consequences, good or bad, are the fruit of the seed we sow. The word *curse* in the original language presents a most intriguing concept of a person who falls under a curse while experiencing the fullness of their desired pursuit, in contradiction to God's prescription for life. A drug addict does not choose to have their teeth fall out, be evicted, or become homeless; a prostitute or thief doesn't intend to lose custody of their children or die from AIDS, but that is the fruit growing from the seed planted.

When we do not choose life, by default, we choose death. Sadly, we convince ourselves we can plant a seed without considering the inevitable fruit of that seed. We want drugs without addiction, gluttony without the weight gain, stress without sickness or pain, immorality without disease, selfishness without the loss of being loved…the list is endless! Choosing the path of death brings us under the curse, not God. The curse is the harvest produced by the seed we have chosen; it is the universal law of sin and death.

In the Book of Romans, Paul tells us we are delivered from the law of sin and death. If we lift that scripture out of context, it can take on a wide variety of meanings. But when put in context of the verse, the book of Romans and the overall word of God, we get a more precise understanding. First of all, that which frees us from the law of sin and death is our choice to operate in the law of the Spirit of life in Christ Jesus. This means we reject the carnal mind that is set on gratifying the desires of the flesh.

It is important to point out, in this same Epistle Paul warns that even though we are Christians, sin still brings death. In Galatians Paul warns believers to stop deceiving themselves: whatever a man sows that shall he also reap: the law of the seed.

When we were sinners by nature, we had no freedom of choice. We were slaves in Egypt, that's all we knew. But now in Christ, we have the Truth; we have the power of the Holy Spirit and we have freedom of choice. But every choice is still a seed and every seed bears fruit after its own kind!

Our understanding of the curse corrupts our interaction with God and our personal role in managing our own life choices. He does not put the curse on us; the curse emerges as a result of our choices. The addict's decision to abuse drugs has made inheriting the Kingdom of God an impossibility. The happiness and fulfillment of the addict are limited to the momentary pleasure of gratifying the flesh. The addict will continue living in the fruit of those choices until new decisions are made (repentance). But because of the life and power of God, the addict can repent at any time, turn to God wholeheartedly and experience true freedom once again.

Repentance is not our attempt to change God's mind. God's mind is made up; regardless of where you are in life, Jesus has already provided a way for you to enter into the Kingdom about what we think He is doing to us. Repentance is when we change our minds about the path we have chosen to walk. Like the father in the story of the prodigal, the father did not cause either the good or the bad consequences experienced by the rebellious son. The consequences were the result of the son's decisions. He could stay in relationship with His father and continue to have access to the father's resources or cut him off from those resources by pursuing fulfillment in another way.

The promise of God is like a map to a buried treasure given by God to warn us of the obstacles we will face along the way. But it also gives us assurances, tools, and insight so we can find and enjoy the treasure. However, if we want the treasure we must follow the map, we will only follow the map if we trust him.

On the path to the treasure there are many ways unbelief can set us off course, giving rise to chaos (evil), and because of the metastatic nature of chaos, it sets us on a course of making one bad decision after another. To add insult to injury, should we find ourselves surrounded by danger, miles from the treasure and time has been lost, we blame God. The children of Israel arrived in Canaan forty years late as a result of their refusal to trust and follow God. This is clearly what happens when at any point we abandon our faith in Him. Thankfully God will not punish us, but it is we who destroy ourselves through the chaos inherited from the path we chose to walk.

I have always found it interesting that people would come to Jesus with all manner of problems. He would minister to them and then set out on His journey. Many of them wanted Him to stay with them. He never stopped moving along His journey; He simply invited them to follow Him in His. We choose to stay where we are and have what that will bring, or we can choose to follow Him and experience whatever benefits exist in His presence. Either way, the choice is ours.

HeartWork

Read This Aloud Before Every HeartWork Session: The Kingdom of God is internal. HeartWork is designed to remove any internal obstacles that prevent me from entering the realm where I experience Heaven on Earth!

1. Do I tend to blame God for the consequences of my actions and decisions?

2. Do I think the consequences of a bad decision is the punishment of God?

3. When I realize I have made a destructive choice do I accept it without guilt or condemnation?

4. When I have made a bad decision, do I look to God's word for a better solution?

CHAPTER 20

I Don't Want to Understand

People tend to misunderstand in a way that always benefits them!

When a person says, "I don't understand." It is difficult to know to what they are referring. Are they saying, "I don't understand why I should do this. I don't understand how I should do this." Or, maybe they're saying, "This makes no sense to me; therefore I refuse to do it." Based on the definition of the word, it is clear that what we do or do not understand can be a reflection of our character and ethics.

One thing I have noticed is this: when people misunderstand they usually misunderstand in a way that benefits them. For example, I've never had anyone misunderstand a business agreement where they paid me more than we agreed. Amazingly, every time there was a misunderstanding about the payment due, they always thought they should pay me less than we agreed. Why does that happen? Simple! Understanding is a matter of the heart.

The Hebrew language defines *hear* and *obey* as the same words. The greatest commandment tells us to hear, which in the mind of the Hebrew believer was *to hear with a readiness to obey*, which meant: to hear and obey was to love God with our entire being. The person who is not willing to obey cannot hear the direction of the Lord. Not hearing may not mean, complete spiritual deafness. It may mean not able to hear clearly and understand. To enter the Kingdom Jesus said we must see AND perceive, hear AND understand.

As already established, the Kingdom of God is a moral Kingdom, not dead works, not works righteousness, not going back under the law. It is a Kingdom where to be a citizen we must be born again of a righteous nation. We must have a repentant teachable heart. The one law that governs every aspect of the Kingdom is: "'You shall love the Lord your God with all your heart, with all your soul, and with all your mind.' This is the first and great commandment. And the second is like it: 'You shall love your neighbor as yourself,'" Matt 22:37-39.

There is a New Testament scripture that says God will not allow anyone into His Kingdom. But there are scriptures that say a person who is committed to a particular lifestyle cannot inherit what Jesus has provided for them. This is why saved, but immoral ungodly, i.e. carnal (natural/fleshly), selfish believers cannot enter in. They don't want to enter in. They do not trust their deepest needs can be fulfilled by walking in God's love and righteousness.

As long as love is defined by unscriptural humanist concepts, everyone raves about love. But those who do not love righteousness have no interest in entering the Kingdom of God. They want all the benefits, but not the personal responsibility of walking in love. Love, as God defines it, is the core of the Gospel; the heart of God's nature. The definition of our character and the motivation of all God has said or done.

The Apostle Paul explained what should be obvious: *faith (trust) works by love* (Gal. 5:6). We cannot trust anyone beyond the love (value) they hold for us. The Apostle John points out, when we do not walk in love it is simply because we are not experiencing love. Love, like many factors of the heart, is a continuum: the love we give cannot be separated from the love we receive (experience). The love that motivates us and in turn, acts upon others through us, is the love that acts upon us.

The Hebrew language has another word for a love that is given, received, and given back. That word is not found in the Greek New Testament since there is no Greek word for this type of reciprocal love. The closest we find is the phrase, *perfect love, love perfected,* or *love completed.* These two Greek words or used to describe the type of love relationship that God seeks with us. Furthermore, it describes not just the love God gives to us, but how that love affects our relationship to others.

Love that is perfected is brought to the goal or fulfillment of its intention. In other words, those who truly experience the love of God bring it to completion, give it back to God, begin to love what God loves, and very specifically loves others. *"If we love one another, God abides in us, and His love has been perfected in us."* (1 John 4:12)

The love to which God has called us is not a selfish endeavor where we seek only to receive love and enjoy the benefits. The love to which God has called us is a love that becomes the core of our character, our motivation, our supreme expression. This love becomes the guiding factor in all we do. Every deep-seated emotional need of mankind is resolved in knowing, feeling and giving God's love.

As we have humanized the Gospel and paganized our definition of love, we have adopted a "faith-free" concept that says: the love of God will change the world. That's not true. If it was, the world would be changed because God already loves the world. For love to transform someone, it must be experienced. For it to be experienced it must be received. For it to be received it must be believed. The only evidence we have that an individual is experiencing God's love is the fruit in their life. *"He who does not love does not know God, for God is love."* (1 John 4:8)

The word "know" in the previous verse is an experiential knowing. It would not be a stretch to say it like this. The person who does not express love is not experiencing love. The question is not, "Does God love me?" The question is, "Do I experience that love; do I feel loved?" This verse reveals the fact that God's love has no benefit or value in our lives until it is experienced, and the only proof of that experience is what we express to Him and the world around us. It is this reciprocal love that drives out fear; it is this relational love that brings forth faith; it is this love that inspires obedience.[1] This love is what compels us to love one another.

The profile of the believer unwilling to obey the commandment to love their neighbor is not typically a viscous blasphemer, perpetrator or career criminal. Defying the command to love our neighbor is more often expressed when we are unwilling to walk in forgiveness or mercy, or when we are divisive or slanderous. As much as anything it is when we are motivated by fear or selfishness rather than love. Why? Because we simply have not yet become disciples. We live by our emotions while deceiving ourselves that we are fully committed to the Lord. These fears or unwillingness to walk in love have to be justified. The very best justification is, "I don't understand."

The resistant believer will nearly always claim they need more explanation or clarification before they can comply to something "as complicated" as walking in love. We can never judge the motive for a person's actions, but my experiences in counseling and personal ministry usually came down to the person not understanding or not wanting to understand. We must remember, however, if we knew and trusted the God of the Word we would trust the Word of God. It seems what we want is justification for refusing to choose God's way of life.

The question, *"Who is my neighbor?"* was presented to Jesus by someone who claimed not to understand these two love commands. It sounds like a reasonable question, but as we learned, confusion is usually the result of selfish ambition.

"For wherever there is jealousy (envy) and contention (rivalry and selfish ambition), there will also be confusion (unrest, disharmony, rebellion) and all sorts of evil and vile practices." (James 3:16, AMP)

When we have predetermined what we will or will not do, we have automatically, by default, negated the capacity to hear and understand with our heart. In the case of the law expert who posed this question in Luke 10:29, we know that his motivation was not to understand, but to *justify himself,* Lk. 10:29.

The desire for understanding is healthy and expected. Over and over again, Proverbs advises us to seek understanding. In fact, along the continuum of knowledge, understanding, and wisdom, a faithful heart that trusts God is the only means by which we can understand. For the heart that does not trust, however, the need to understand is a form of testing God. We are essentially putting Him on trial to prove Himself beyond what He has already proven in Christ. By exercising our determination of what is right and wrong, we judge God and His Word, and on some level, believe we are more just, righteous and fair than God. We require an explanation so we can determine whether or not we think He is right or wrong.

The disciple, however, trusts Jesus' representation of God's character, His interpretation of God's commandments, and His teaching about faith and love as the motive for application of God's truth. The disciple believes that quality of life is based on two factors: the degree to which we experience God through Jesus determines the quality of our inner life, and the degree we walk in love, as defined by God's commandments, determines the quality of our interrelationships. Out of a faith-filled heart, the disciple experiences the grace of God, the power of the Holy Spirit, the resurrection life. A repentant, teachable heart hears, understands, believes and receives, even in the absence of doctrinal definitions because it is a heart phenomenon, not an intellectual comprehension.

One of the first laws of the Kingdom is found in the parable of the pearl of great price where the objective is clear: to get this magnificent pearl we must be ready to give up all else. The pearl is not accessible to us unless we want God and Kingdom life more than anything else. When we do not want the Kingdom more than anything else, we will face the same fate as in the parable of the sower. However, when we believe we have the opportunity for life at its best, we cannot be drawn away or deceived. What we hear will resonate in the deepest part of our being; we will walk a path that cannot be explained, but rather, experienced. We will have a connection to God that is more valuable than anything else in life. We will experience a peace that makes no sense for which our heart will continually rejoice!

HeartWork

Read This Aloud Before Every HeartWork Session: The Kingdom of God is internal. HeartWork is designed to remove any internal obstacles that prevent me from entering the realm where I experience Heaven on Earth!

1. Can I honestly say: I seek the Kingdom of God and His righteousness because of all things?

2. When I am unsure of the "right" thing, do I first seek to treat the other person fairly, or do I first determine what will meet my needs?

3. Am I afraid treating the other person fairly will cause me to somehow lose?

CHAPTER 21

Walking in the Spirit

Truth is always absolute, but the application of truth is always variable.

The Pentecostal influence on the doctrine of the Holy Spirit tended to define exaggerated emotional phenomenon as signs and wonders. They, like Israel, wanted to see the miracles, signs, and wonders more than they wanted to know God intimately. Sadly, many of the Pentecostal extremes, combined with very poor scriptural interpretation caused the orthodox church to become even more opposed to the ministry of the Holy Spirit.

The Charismatics brought the ministry of the Holy Spirit another step forward with a primary emphasis of the gifts of the Spirit. But it seemed, once again, the main pursuit was the gifts, not the Giver. An overemphasis on speaking in tongues was both an attraction to some of the church world but was equally repelling to many.

More mainline denominations, like Baptists and Methodist, acknowledged the presence of the Holy Spirit, but any manifestation was shunned and often attributed to the devil. What seemed to lack in every group was an emphasis on the power of the Holy Spirit to manifest the character and nature of God in our lives. Historically, the church, like Israel has sought eternal manifestations and minimized internal godliness.

Interestingly in the early seventies, the Southern Baptist denomination embraced the fruit of the Spirit, but vehemently rejected all other biblically-based manifestations of the Holy Spirit. It was not uncommon for those who spoke in tongues or prayed for the sick to be expelled from their local congregation. But even more confusing was the acceptance and embracing of the fruit of the Spirit but absolutely no teaching on the subject. The Baptists, like many other denominations, were Calvinistic in their doctrine. Thus, embracing a doctrine meant: if God wants something to manifest in your life He'll make it happen.

For the last 50-60 years. Pentecostal, Charismatic and Word of Faith teachers, have seen and preached the promises. Where the water became too mirky to follow was in the area of application. Most of what we were taught about application was formula based. As often as not, it was someone telling their personal story, attempting to persuade the listener to emulate their journey, i.e., formula. The problem with formulas is they have no allowance for the personal beliefs of the heart, the leadership of the Holy Spirit, nor do they allow for the millions of variables which can be present in two seemingly similar situations.

One of the greatest deceptions in formula-based ministry is sometimes they actually work. When there are enough similarities in two people's situation, they may be able to produce a similar outcome in both situations. This gives a false proof that the formula works. Once people believe in the formula, they stop trusting in God, His promise and the finished work of Jesus; they work the formula. It allows no room for God to lead a person in the way they should walk.

Truth is absolute, but the application is 100% variable. Sadly, the average Christian in America seems more committed to their method of application than the truth they seek to apply. In my experience, I see many godly people who believe God's promise, they know it is theirs through the finished work of Jesus, yet they are incapable of hearing God in the midst of their life-storm. They don't know how to walk with the Holy Spirit in the way He is leading them! They pay more attention to the people speaking into their lives than the voice of God speaking in their heart!

One of the most repeated phrases in the New Testament is, *"to him who has ears to hear, let him hear."* Why is this verse repeated so often? Simple! Once we believe the truth as presented in the life, teaching, death, burial, and resurrection of Jesus, the only thing lacking to live in the promise is hearing and following the Holy Spirit. The repentant, teachable heart of a disciple hears because he or she has predetermined to obey. Therefore they hear. As previously discussed we can/will only hear that which we are willing to obey, i.e. put into practice.

The twenty-third Psalm is one of the most quoted and memorized passages in the Bible. But evidently, it is one of the least believed. If the Lord is our Shepherd, and the 23rd Psalm describes where and how He leads us, why do we not believe and live by this Psalm? Since the Lord is our Shepherd, we can be sure He always attempts to lead us in the path of Life! He leads us away from lack, and He leads us to a place of peace, provision, protection, and security! If I want to find myself in still waters, green pastures, righteousness, freedom from fear and a victory cel-ebration the ultimate key is to follow His leadership. If we believe this, our first effort in resolving any problem would be to get alone, into our heart and listen for the direction of our Great Shepherd. He will always lead us to the solution.

The Spirit of God is the Spirit of Wisdom. Wisdom is always related to practical application; therefore the Spirit of Wisdom will always lead us into the practical application of truth. When a promise of God is not manifesting there are only three possible reasons:

1. Unbelief
2. Doubt (wavering)
3. Disobedience.

Unbelief is when we do not believe the truth of what Jesus accomplished. Doubt is to choose or vacillate between two beliefs. 3) disobedience is either the inabil-ity to hear and follow the Holy Spirit or the unwillingness to trust and follow the Holy Spirit. When we cannot/do not hear the voice of Wisdom we default to a formula or to something we have tried in the past!

As discussed previously, one of the greatest fears of mankind is the fear of the un-known. Researchers tell us, the mind takes everything it hears and compares it to all of our life experiences. This is why people suffer from PTSD and similar fears or phobias. A veteran of war, hears a car backfire and the mind says, this sounds like an explosion. Before they can rationally process the information they react. Thus, their reaction is irrational to the casual observer. All past experiences that negatively affect us today are a form of PTSD. The mind is saying, "this is that."

It appears, when we have a great opportunity, beyond the scope of our previous experiences, our mind looks for those similarities. When they cannot be found, it tends to move us into doing this "new thing" the way we have done things in the past. This is one of the factors that keeps us repeating our mistakes. We don't want to venture into the unknown. Instead of focusing on the One who is lead-ing us down the path we focus on the path. We'll change the terminology, rear-range certain aspects of application, but that's a bait and switch. We will eventu-ally try what we've tried before, even though it didn't work the first time, and then be surprised when it doesn't work this time. We'll convince ourselves we are following God, but the truth is we are following the path that makes sense to us.

Among godly, people sincerely seeking God's solutions this may be the main reason they do not see the promise manifest as it should. We are facing a disaster, but in our hearts, we know God has already met this need in Jesus. Then the Holy Spirit speaks to our heart to assure us of God's promise. We are right on track... but that's when we kick into carnal control mode. Rather than face the insecurity of walking an unknown path, we gratefully thank God for what He is showing us, and then in as kind of a way as possible, inform Him, "I'll take it from here!"

It is one thing to believe God for the promise, but it is a different thing to trust Him in a process that is foreign or simply unknown to us. We must remember, in every situation, there are too many variables for us to recognize them, and it's even harder when the variables are changing daily. But God is all-knowing! He knows everything that is changing; He knows everything about everyone involved; He knows what's coming next; therefore He can lead you through the process. But we want Him to explain the process. Why? We don't trust Him. We want to put Him on trial and judge Him by our perspective and knowledge.

Our past experience defines how we can manifest the miracle we need, while still feeling safe. Now, instead of following the Holy Spirit and walking the path where He is leading, we want to walk the path we trust. We want Him to come to our path and bless our decision, rather than walk the path He is walking. We are in total disharmony with the Holy Spirit but somehow convince ourselves we will end up at the same destination. We convince ourselves, "since I believe the promise, I am walking in/with the Spirit."

When the Bible tells us to walk in the Spirit an array of mental pictures come to mind, all of which reveal what it means to walk in the Spirit. One concept of walking in the Spirit is to yoke up with Him, like pairs of oxen that must keep in step to pull the load. There is, however a picture within this picture, that makes the metaphor even more clear and simple. Walking together actually speaks of getting into harmony. In other words, walking in the Spirit is when we harmo- nize our choices with His when we trust what He is doing enough to get in sync and follow.

God is always leading us down a path that our heart can trust. We're like a person standing on the bank of a river looking at the solution to our problem on the other bank. Based on our perception we look across the river see the treasure we seek and decide, let's cross the river. God says, "but there are crocodiles in the riv- er.' You reply, "that's not a problem you can make me walk on water." God knows you lack the faith to walk on water, especially if you see the Crocodiles. So, He seeks to lead you another way, a journey He knows you can make. You, however, insist on crossing the river, because you trust your way more than God's. Good luck with those crocodiles!

God is attempting to, not merely bring us into particular, individual promises. He is seeking to bring us into this realm called the Kingdom of God. In this realm, we don't wait until there is a problem and then try to get delivered from it. In this realm, we live in the promises and avoid the problems. This is a way of life that is only possible when we walk in the Spirit, thereby avoiding the lusts of the flesh. This is a way of life that depends on the Spirit of grace to empower our righteous nature.

We sometimes forget that Kingdom living is not just righteousness, peace and joy, but it is righteous, peace and joy in the Holy Spirit. This is an internal destination that can only be found by harmonizing with the Holy Spirit: listening to His voice and follow in His footsteps. In a prophecy to Israel about living in the Promised Land, we see what has its ultimate fulfillment in the Kingdom of God. *"I will put My Spirit within you and cause you to walk in My statutes, and you will keep My judgments and do them. Then you shall dwell in the land that I gave to your fathers."* (Ez. 36:27-28)

Since we know God's names and His promises, we know where God is leading. What we don't know is the path He will take to get us there. The path is the way; we want a way that is familiar to us; we want to put our faith in the path/process. In our journey into Kingdom living, i.e. living in personal intimacy with God and enjoying access to all His resources, we will put our faith in the path (process) or the one who leads us on the path. One way is the tree of life; the other is the knowledge of good and evil as we see it! Which one makes you feel safe?

HeartWork

Read Every time: The Kingdom of God is internal. HeartWork is designed to remove any internal obstacles that prevent me from entering the realm where I experience Heaven on Earth!

1. What comes to my mind when I think of walking in the Spirit?

2. Do I ever recognize the voice of God speaking or leading me?

3. Do I trust God is always leading me to the very best life possible?

4. Am I uncomfortable when I feel lead, to walk a path that is foreign to me?

5. Would I like to go through a free mentoring program to get a better grasp on how to walk with God? Visit: https://www.impactministries.com/living-under-lordship/ to learn more.

CHAPTER 22

The Secret Place

The first door to the secret place is my heart; the second door is God's heart!

Ps 91 begins with one of the most endearing and alluring statements in the Bible: *"He who dwells in the secret place of the Most High, shall abide under the shadow of the Almighty."* I have heard hours of discussion about the secret place, what it is, where it is and how one finds it. Regardless of the academic discussion, every believer seeking intimacy with God feels a tug on their heartstrings when this verse is read. I think like, so many Spiritual realities, we over-think or over define this. Secret place means: to be hidden or to be concealed.[1] Like many Hebrew words, the concept is more important than the theological translation.

The root Hebrew word translated as "secret place" is spelled Samek, Taw, Resh. Samek is a circle representing being concealed, protected and covered over by God. Taw represents God's absolute truth, and Resh is a picture of being led by the Holy Spirit, facilitated by our repentant heart. This is a picture of being in a secret, special place and time with God, receiving truth for our lives that leads to a divine perfection.

Based on other scriptures about God's intimacy, especially from the Song of Solomon. One could easily conclude the secret place to be where one takes His lover to share in secret that which is not for anyone else to see, hear. In this place, He shares His secrets and plans for the one who has stolen His heart with her love. He speaks to her about what He longs to give her. He assures her of His

1   From The Online Bible Thayer's Greek Lexicon and Brown Driver & Briggs Hebrew Lexicon, Copyright © 1993, Woodside Bible Fellowship, Ontario, Canada. Licensed from the Institute for Creation Research.

protection. The secret place is a heart-to-heart connection only shared by those who love one another deeply, openly and honestly! They hold nothing back! This is a picture of a reciprocal love, God desires with all His children.

Because of His love, God is always attempting to connect deeply and personally, wherein He shares His heart with us, and gives us wisdom needed to remediate our current dilemmas, help us avoid future struggles, keep us from harm and provide loving, protective guidance. But this is something He shares in private, in our times of intimacy. Many times God would call the children of Israel to sanctify themselves, i.e. set themselves apart for time with Him. It would be in these times that they would receive incredibly important revelation about upcoming events. It was usually in time of "being set apart" when the prophets would receive important revelation about the future.

This call to intimacy is built on a fourth Hebrew word for love. There was no single word for this love in the Greek, nor in the English. This word in the Hebrew language is used of a love that is shared; it is reciprocal. In the Greek New Testament, the Greek word agape is used to describe the kind of love God gives. However, agape is not a word that describes a reciprocal love relationship. It is a quality of love that God gives because of His character. It is the kind of love we are called to give, as well. Agape is a selfless love, that is not conditional. Those to whom, this love is given may or may not receive it, but it is still given. It is this love of God that prevents Him from pouring out His wrath and judgment on the earth at this time. It is this type of love that, because of its unwavering nature can eventually draw a person to repentance. But it is not a relational, reciprocal love.

In recent years shallow theologians have tried to imply that the agape of God is such a quality of love that we need not love Him back, to enjoy the benefits of His love. This leads to the error of universalism, ultimate reconciliation and other false doctrines that teach there is no need for personal faith or relationship. They misconstrue God's love to be so great He will violate one's will to give them what He desires. They forget that faith and love are the key components of a relationship. Thus, the opposite is true, because God is love He will never violate your free will. You can have the life you choose, even if it destroys you. He will try to warn and redirect you, but if you reject Him, He will never force you. Love is never expressed through control!

Since the Greek has no one word to express the Hebrew word for love reciprocated it uses two words which are usually translated as perfect love or love completed. These words are referring to the Hebrew word that is used to describe a shared love between two people. In other words, God's agape love has not reached its ultimate goal until it is believed, experienced and given back to God and to the world. This is the love relationship to which all are called, but few respond.

John 3:16 says For God so loved, from the Greek "agapeo." Agape describes God's selfless love. This is a love that flows from His character; it is not the expression of a relationship. This incredible love of God does not, however, benefit anyone until it is believed, received and experienced. As I have previously stated, if God loving us is all we need, the entire world would be saved, healed and enjoying heaven on earth, because He already loves the world. God's love is not a factor for most of the world because they reject it, or attempt to take advantage of it.

I often hear people say, love drives out fear. Technically, that's not what that passage says. It says perfect love casts out fear, i.e., love experienced. I love the way it reads in the NLT: "... *perfect love expels all fear. If we are afraid, it is for fear of punishment, and this shows that we have not fully experienced his perfect love.*" (1 John 4:18-19) It is only after we personally experience His love that we free ourselves from the fear of Him hurting us, which is the prerequisite for faith (trust). After all, *faith works by love.* We can only fully trust the one who through his character and His promises, and our personal involvement we know He has no intent to hurt us. A lack of personal interaction has rendered most people completely unaware of God's love.

This intimate knowledge of God begins with knowing Him through what He has chosen to reveal to all mankind: the Bible. The Bible is the revealed knowledge of God. More than any place in the Bible, God's love is revealed in the death, burial and resurrection of the Lord Jesus, 1 John 4:9-11. This proactive, preemptive sacrifice to a world that doesn't deserve it is God's ultimate expression of His. It is His call to the entire world to trust Him and come to Him!

As mentioned previously, every letter in the Hebrew Alphabet has its own meaning. When translating and interpreting a word, one step in the process is to look up the meanings of each of the letters in the root word. The definitions of the three root letters become part of the overall interpretation of every Hebrew word.

One very interesting Hebrew letter is called MEM and is obviously where we get the *M* sound. The original symbol even looks somewhat like an M. There are two different MEMs, both having to do with *knowledge*. The caveat is that the second type of knowledge is personal and intimate. We'll discuss it in the next chapter. To understand the second MEM we must understand the first.

The MEM represents the knowledge of God. The first MEM looks like a rectangle standing on its end with the left bottom corner slightly open, symbolizing this knowledge is revealed, or poured out to the world, through the Word of God. We sometimes forget that the first five books of the Bible, known as the Pentateuch or Torah, are the Words spoken directly by God Himself. They are not, in fact, the inspirational words of a prophet but actual direct quotes made by God. All subsequent biblical truth is based on the Torah, and anyone who

1	Holy Bible, New Living Translation ®, copyright © 1996, 2004 by Tyndale Charitable Trust. Used by permission of Tyndale House Publishers. All rights reserved.

rejects these words rejects God's testimony of Himself.

In modern church terminology, we often hear the phrase, *revelation knowledge*, which in our church culture represents the idea of a special revelation from God. Unfortunately, modern Christianity has moved so far away from what God Himself spoke from His own mouth that we embrace the idea of a progressive revelation of God. Catholics believe in the Pope's infallibility and power to speak Ex Cathedra, which is a self-appointed authority that gives him the right to reinterpret or replace the written Word of God.

Charismatics and Pentecostals, who condemn such doctrine in Catholicism, will receive a personal prophecy, or word of knowledge incongruent with the Word of God and base their faith on its fulfillment. Universalists and other inclusionist and New Agers believe, like the early Gnostics, their personal revelations of God are as reliable and relevant as anything in the Bible. Carnal believers, despite what the Word of God says, believe their personal experience and subjective interpretations are equal to the Word of God. When we do not believe and receive the Word of God as taught, modeled, and revealed through the life, teachings, death, burial, and resurrection of Jesus, we are subscribing to our personal version of revelation knowledge, not God's. Revelation knowledge is not a special or private revelation; it is what God has revealed in His Word. It seems every group has some way to twist the Word of God to their personal preference and justify it!

Our connection to God is heart to heart; it is relational and, like all intimate relationships, it is built on love, truth, and trust. A dimension of intimate knowledge and personal revelation between God and the believer does exist, but it never violates or rejects what God has previously stated. When our revelation is not in the Bible, incongruent with the Bible, or in opposition to the Bible, it is a deception. Intimate knowledge and personal revelation are never experienced by the person who rejects God's revealed knowledge: the first MEM.

At some point, we must decide our attitude toward God's Word. "Do I believe the testimony God has given of Himself?" If my response is positive, the next questions is, do I want to move from intellectual knowledge to more personal application? If my response is negative, I have made God a liar. There can be no intimate relationship with one I consider to be a liar, myth or some part of my imagination.

The letter MEM represents water. In the ancient world, water has always been represented a mystery. One could stand on the shore or, in a boat, see the surface of the water and occasionally a few feet beneath the surface. But everyone knew there were mysteries hidden beneath the surface. One could stand on the shore and speculate all that lay beneath the surface, but that was just theory. But the serious-minded could dive into the water to discover the mysteries for themselves.

God's revealed knowledge is like that water; we can stand on the shore and spec-

125

ulate, or we can dive in to discover for ourselves what God longs to say to every living human being. This revealed knowledge that becomes experiential knowledge is what leads us to know the truth of God and His love for mankind. It is the starting place of what can become a deep intimate relationship wherein we hear the voice of God in our heart!

Kingdom living is not theory, and it is not mere information. *For the Kingdom of God is not just a lot of talk; it is living by God's power,*[1] 1 Cor 4:20. Entering the Kingdom realm through the door of the heart is the place where faith finds its full expression, involvement becomes relationship as one experiences the Secret Place of God. In this place, we internally live, move and have our being in a realm that cannot be seen or heard, by those who do not experience it!

1   Holy Bible, New Living Translation ®, copyright © 1996, 2004 by Tyndale Charitable Trust. Used by permission of Tyndale House Publishers. All rights reserved.

HeartWork

Read Every Time: The Kingdom of God is internal. HeartWork is designed to remove any internal obstacles that prevent me from entering the realm where I experience Heaven on Earth!

1. Do I desire to find and enter the secret place of God?

2. Do I set aside time for Bible study, prayer, and meditation?

3. Even though I may not understand it, do I accept God's Word as the only basis for the knowledge of God?

4. List five things you are doing to develop your faith (trust for God).

5. What is my plan to daily interact with God?

CHAPTER 23

Being Taught of the Lord

Will you know about your spouse's love by a passionate kiss or reading your marriage license?

The determining factor for how our walk with the Lord progresses is based on how the journey is started and the destination chosen. The world is growing more lawless and less teachable. With the rise of lawlessness worldwide, the failure of parents to teach children personal responsibility, humanistic philosophy taught in our schools, political correctness reverberating in our halls of government, and the continual seduction for self-gratification equals a vast majority of people who may realize their need for Christ but are rarely ready for Kingdom living. We are a generation of people who want relief without the effort of resolving problems!

Many believers start their journey with God resistant to the fundamental truths that bring about salvation. In the name of freedom, new Christians seldom surrender their personal opinions but rather approach God's Word as a judge who decides if the evidence is enough to prove the case. The two truths involved in the born-again experience are: believe in your heart that God raised Jesus from the dead, and confess Him as Lord.

Our identity is a factor of the heart. The only way to put on our new identity in Christ is to believe in and join in His resurrection. Few believers every establish a sense of their new identity, that's why they struggle their entire life with the sins and temptations of the old man. Even fewer ever commit to Jesus as Lord; therefore they cannot experience His grace working in their heart to live in righteousness. Even more devastating is this: in the absence of a commitment to Lordship the new believer is not a disciple, they are not repentant and teachable, they cling to their personal opinion and live in lawlessness. It seems the modern salvation message is something like: "Hey Would you like a free ticket to heaven?"

Lawlessness, or as the KJV translates it, *iniquity*, is the core evil that launched the rebellion of Lucifer and will earmark the rise of the antichrist, bringing about the final rebellion at the end of the Millennium. Between the beginning and end of this rebellion, every woe that has come, and will come upon mankind, is the result of iniquity. The word *iniquity* literally means *no law*, and launches the rejection or twisting of God's prescriptive commands, replacing them with humanistic philosophies. One of the earmarks of the last days is that love will grow cold. The commandments teach us how to treat people with love, but in the current humanist culture, love is no longer defined by God's Word; it is replaced with an insidious infection that defines love as nothing more than permissiveness and self-indulgence. This corrupt definition is a bold declaration that says, *"I am more just, more fair, and more righteous than God. My opinion is more reliable than His Word."*

Salvation means *to be saved, healed, delivered, blessed, prospered, protected, made whole, i.e., all the promises of the Kingdom*, and it starts with the heart-belief that God raised Jesus from the dead - not just physical death, but death according to the Scriptures. We are easily compelled to surrender to His Lordship when we embrace the belief that Jesus, through His resurrection, conquered death, sin, hell, the devil, and obtained eternal life for us.

The word *confess* literally means *to say the same thing*. Confession is not, however, a mere recitation of the words, *Jesus is Lord*; it is saying the same thing Scripture says about His death, burial, and resurrection with our heart in full agreement. Jesus is not just Lord, *Jesus is my Lord!* By making Him Lord, we are making a choice to follow Him in His interpretation of God's Word, His representation of God's character, and His manifestation of God's love at the cross.

Yielding to Lordship is the doorway of salvation that leads to the path of discipleship. The concept of Lordship is almost extinct in many forms of modern Christianity, although the empty words are quoted by religious workers of iniquity daily. *Lordship* is, by default, *a decision for discipleship that leads to an interactive relationship*. Through this interaction, we experience the reality of God's Word, producing inward changes that manifest in how we manage our lives. As we believe and apply truth, our character changes and our relationships flourish. Chaos (evil) is replaced with peace. Even those in hostile environments who are persecuted for their faith, experience a peace that passes understanding. The more we *taste and see that the Lord is good,* the more we value Him and His sacrifice, the more we love the wisdom of His Word, and the more we develop intimacy. This is the way of the disciple.

Disciples do not read the Bible from obligation nor do they try to live godly to appease or earn anything from God. Disciples are in an interactive love relationship - a reciprocity of giving and receiving that places them in the unique position for continuous communication with God in their heart. By evaluating all that is heard in light of Jesus, disciples are in an ever-ready state of trustful obedience (yielding) to the truth.

The open MEM introduced in the last chapter represents the revealed knowledge of God given to all mankind. The second is the closed MEM. It looks just like the first except for the fact that its bottom left-hand corner is closed, signifying *secret knowledge*. This knowledge, as it is in the Greek New Testament, is *experiential*, not merely intellectual. To know God refers to the capacity of the heart, soul, mind, and body to experience intimacy. It is not a subjective or *private interpretation* of God's revealed knowledge, but an application of His wisdom that imparts personal leadership in decision-making. Experiential knowledge is a whisper from the mouth of God that cannot be expressed in words but is imprinted onto and understood with our heart, just as that which transpires between two lovers in their most intimate moments. It is not for preaching or sharing—it is for living!

The top of the MEM looks like waves of water. Water, in all ancient cultures, was mysterious. One could look at the top of the water and see some of the life just below the surface. As previously stated, to truly know the secrets of the deep, one must dive in and see for themselves. All others stand at a distance and theorize concerning what is held in the deep. This is the difference between a student and a disciple. This level of intimate sharing is the difference between happens among friends and what happens among lovers!

Scriptures in the Old and New Testaments depict God's relationship with the believer as a deep, loving intimacy between a husband and wife, but not just any wife. As Chaim Bentorah[1] points out in his excellent teaching of the Hebrew language, in ancient times men often had more than one wife. Just the fact that a man would bring a woman into his home, provide for her, and have children with her would represent a level of love. But quite often, he would have one wife that had stolen his heart. She was the one he adored. This is the passionate relationship described throughout the Song of Solomon.

You have ravished my heart, My sister, my spouse; You have ravished my heart With one look of your eyes, With one link of your necklace. How fair is your love, My sister, my spouse! How much better than wine is your love, And the scent of your perfumes Than all spices! Your lips, O my spouse, Drip as the honeycomb; Honey and milk are under your tongue; And the fragrance of your garments Is like the fragrance of Lebanon. A garden enclosed Is my sister, my spouse, Song 4:9-12.

The mysterious *secret place* of God is where we experience an intimacy and trust that cannot be conveyed in mere words. The favored wife could find that *secret place* when returning the same genuine love to her husband. Jesus referred to some believers who experience instruction and leadership that is not common to all believers. The legalist would interpret this as favoritism or partiality, but this is because they approach God from the basis of a contract, not a relationship.

All born-again believers are the Bride of Christ. The same offer of intimacy and involvement has been extended to all, and it is an unconditional offer. We have all been received by the Groom, and we all have the promises extended to us. Not all believers, however, have entered into intimacy and reciprocal love where those promises are shared and experienced. Grace is the power, capacity, strength, and ability, given without merit, expressed from the heart, that makes us able to do and be all God says we are. The modern *Grace Movement* tends to think grace is experienced by the person who knows the doctrine of grace. However, as the word implies, grace works in and through the heart. It is a power that is exchanged in the intimacy of giving and receiving love. The strength to be who God says we are is the direct result of experiencing who we are unto Him and with Him.

Believers who pray, meditate, and listen (to obey), hear and access the promises of God that others do not, are those who seek God Himself, more than what God has to offer. The difference is made clear in the event of Mary and Martha who both loved Jesus: *Mary chose that good part* (Luke 10:41-42), to be close to the Lord, while Martha chose to be busy with the details. And, again, in the parable of the prodigal son, Jesus explains how the father did not show prejudice to the elder son while the younger son rebelled. The elder son experienced the benefits of closeness, not through perfection or earned benefits, but simply because he remained in fellowship with the father. We vainly expect the "deeper" realities of God to be the result of studying or serving. Both of those are valuable and essential, but they are not relational. I know who I am to my wife because of what we share through our intimate connection. Likewise, our connection to God is a relationship. Who we are to Him grows from our personal involvement and intimacy.

The Zoe life of God is experienced. It is transmitted heart to heart, not brain to brain. Sometimes we get busy doing things for God, or, as is too often the case, the bulk of our involvement with God is to get what we need. We never have that private experience of exchanging our heart; we use Him to meet our needs. How often do we really commune with God just because we want to know Him better or experience a deeper, intimate closeness?

Many times Brenda and I will lie in bed and hold one another for no reason other than the desire to experience closeness. In those moments, our relationship is strengthened, and we experience a love that is not expressed in words. We share the secret knowledge that is only for us. The closed MEM represents what God

131

imprints on our hearts when we are connected and intimate, experiencing the loving uniqueness of our relationship.

HeartWork

Read Every Time: The Kingdom of God is internal. HeartWork is designed to remove any internal obstacles that prevent me from entering the realm where I experience Heaven on Earth!

1. Write a description of your relationship with the Lord.

2. Make a list of what you know and believe about the death, burial, and resurrection of Jesus and the Scriptures upon which you base those beliefs.

3. Write a few paragraphs about how you would like to hear, know, and experience the leadership of God

4. Have you ever made an absolute commitment to Jesus as Lord?

CHAPTER 24

The Truth That Sets Free

Freedom is useless to the man who intends on staying in prison!

The pursuit of "truth" has been corrupted since man's rebellion in the garden. Man lived in paradise; there was no sin, sickness, disease or death. In other words, there was no kind of lack! Man lived in perfect harmony with God, one another and the earth. By means of the serpent, Lucifer, like a corrupt politician deceived man and destroyed Paradise. He then criticized God for what man and the world became. Then the destroyer promised to fix the problem by bringing man knowledge.

So, man somehow believed the one who caused the problem could somehow fix the problem. Why was the human race so vulnerable to such a ridiculous lie? Simple! They were deceived by their lusts. The destroyer promised man could live in his lusts, selfishness, and carnality and still have the Paradise God had once given. Nothing has changed in nearly 6000 years of recorded human history! Man is still attempting to find his way back to Paradise without surrendering to God's wisdom.

This pursuit of the Utopian world comes from the very core of our being. We were created to live in paradise. We have no capacity to abide in physical or emotional distress. We were given a nervous system that avoids pain and seeks pleasure. We are designed to end chaos and return to peace as quickly as possible. Failure to do so introduces death, i.e., we begin to die when we are not in peace. However, because of what man did to the world through his rebellion, there can be no Utopia, paradise or externally manifested Kingdom of God until the earth is purged of those who do not want the Kingdom of God.[1]

The strength of every con man is to play on the victim's greed, i.e. desire! Mankind wants Paradise, but we have come to believe fulfilling the lust of the flesh, the lust of the eyes and the pride of life is the only way to find that happiness. That is our greed. The con is this: there is a way to have paradise and never give up these destructive tendencies. It is no longer the wicked who believe this lie; there is a massive part of the church that has twisted the truth and convinced themselves they can have, paradise and sin!

We must keep in mind, the root of sin and the message of satanism is self-gratification. When we do not believe and experience what we have in God, we feel lack, insufficient and unfulfilled. If we do not believe the truth about God, we will not look to Him to meet these needs. We will use other people to gratify our flesh and our ego!

The humanistic promise of Utopia is to cast off the restraints of morality and gratify yourself. Evidently, no one has "done the math." If everyone is using others for gratification then what you have is not paradise, you have war, abuse, and constant conflict. It is only Utopia for those who have the power to rule over, and abuse others.

Our need for Paradise is legitimate and God-given. But it can only be had by walking in God's definitions of love and justice as spelled out in His commandments. In fact, the person who yields to righteousness or walks in love will, according to Paul, fulfill the commandments, Gal 5:14.

Lucifer and his followers, which include many religious and political philosophies, claim the way to peace and fulfillment is to cast off moral restraints and superstitious beliefs in God. If you do believe in God, then you must realize He is the problem in planet earth. Their corrupt message of sovereignty says He is in control, therefore the mess the world is in shows He is not good and cannot be trusted.

Their argument says, man was bound to the Creator who used His commandment to control by guilt. Lucifer presents himself as the true savior of mankind because he gave man knowledge which set him free from the oppressive Creator. So, the way to this Utopian Paradise is enlightenment, i.e. unique secret knowledge passed down from generation to generation to the elite, who reject God's morals, values, and ethics. Unfortunately, when most people talk about searching for the truth, it may be more accurate to say they are searching for knowledge. Specifically, they are searching for the knowledge to provide the Paradise God promises without adhering to God's morals, values, and ethics as expressed in His commandments. Through their knowledge of love (selfish gratification),

---

1   For a full understanding of why Jesus has to return and when He can return read my book: Apocalypse: A Spiritual Guide to the Second Coming

they reject love as God has defined it!

Among Christians, revelation from God is defined as getting a revelation that is doctrinally correct. It's more about being doctrinally right or wrong than about how to live or treat others. I'll hear preachers say, *I used to think this Scripture meant ....., but now God has shown me it really means ....* It seems that very little of our theology is focused on knowing and walking with God; it's about being doctrinally correct. Unintentionally, we like the Luciferians are in the pursuit of knowledge more than truth.

Jesus addressed the religious study of the Scripture as opposed to a relational approach. *"You search the Scriptures, for in them you think you have eternal life; and these are they which testify of Me. But you are not willing to come to Me that you may have life."* (John 5:39) This leaves us to ask ourselves, "What am I looking for in the scripture? Am I looking for some secret knowledge that will finally open the doors to heaven, or am I looking to know God through the Lord Jesus?" After all, knowledge does not give life. That is the promise of Lucifer: knowledge will produce life! Life comes from knowing and experiencing the only true God and Jesus Christ whom He sent, Jn. 17:3.

Like many believers, the person making such a statement doesn't realize God is trying to speak to them as someone with whom He shares deep personal love. They think He's trying to get their knowledge "right," but He may be attempting to show him its practical application in his present situation. Rather than the previous view being wrong versus the new revelation being right, the previous understanding was how to apply that truth in the situation he was facing at that time. If that person is following the Lord as a disciple, they have to consider what God whispers in their heart as the truth they need for victory in this moment!

Reading the Word of God and prayer should be about connecting to God personally, listening for the whisper of the Lord to lead us into the life He has for us it is not a theology class. There is a time and place to study the Word to understand theology, but not in personal reading and prayer. In our pursuit of Zoe, we need to connect to and EXPERIENCE God in the secret place as we share our heart, one with another. In that intimacy God, via the Holy Spirit, will show us what we need to know about life in this moment. The Holy Spirit does lead us into truth, but we often fail to realize the different aspects as well as the various words for *truth*. There is truth that stands in opposition to error; absolute truth that stands in opposition to a partial truth; and truth for life, its specific challenges and choices at this moment in time.

The Ancients said there are *seventy faces* to the Torah[1]. While there may be one ultimate translation, there can be seventy different aspects to the truth of a single

---

1   Bentorah, Chaim (2014-06-25). Hebrew Word Study: Beyond The Lexicon. Trafford Publishing. Kindle Edition.

word. The Word of God is true, no matter what God shows us, it does not become more true. That which was true was used for thousands of years to oppress and control instead of giving life. When Jesus came and showed us what the facts, i.e. that which was true would look like when applied from the motive of love, when used to heal the hurting and set the captives free, that's when we recognize the truth hidden in that which was true.

In the Hebrew language, the root of every word is a verb, not a noun. Not one Word of God can be understood until it is applied with the intention for which God spoke the Word: to bring forth life! If I interpret and thereby apply any Word of God for any reason other than bringing life to the hearer it is not truth. After Jesus said, My words are life (Zoe)! Therefore, until I take God's Word into my heart and apply as a means of connecting to God and His life, it is not yet truth to me. It may be a formula; it may be a rule, and it may be good advice, but it is not yet truth to me!

Jesus said, *My sheep hear my voice and follow me.* If the ability to hear is contingent on the intention to obey, this Scripture refers to those who are surrendered, not to those who are merely saved offering only conditional obedience. We want to know the truth and recognize the voice of God so we can follow Him as our Shepherd - who always leads us to green pastures, still waters, a banqueting table, and harmony with Him. One of the characteristics of the wisdom of God is it always leads us on a path that ensures our relationship with Him will remain intact.

The revealed knowledge of God is available to us when we seek it, as we study His Word and through the processes of translation and interpretation. The second phase of this process is *secret knowledge* - the last step to translating, interpreting but mainly listening, sensing, perceiving how the Scripture should be applied at this very moment, in our unique situation.

When challenged to prove His doctrine was from God, Jesus said, *"If anyone wills to do His will, he shall know concerning the doctrine, whether it is from God or whether I speak on My own."* (John 7:17) In today's vernacular, that could be said this way, *When you intend to put this into practice, then you will know if your doctrine (interpretation) is based on God's truth.* Truth that is not applied is indistinguishable from theory. Even if that theory can be intellectually or theologically proven to be correct, it is meaningless if not applied from God's true intention: to improve our quality of life.

In John 8:28-29, Jesus reemphasized the fact that He was here speaking the Father's Words from His true intention and doing the Father's works. Remember, the religious world of Jesus' day had turned God's commandments from prescriptions for life and love into commandments that bind and control. For all practical purposes, He was saying, until you see God as I represent Him, you don't see in God. Until you believe in God the way I represent Him, you don't believe in God.

Then in John 8:31-32, He makes one statement that is continually lifted out of context and misquoted. "The truth shall make you free." That phrase is found within a very important statement, but when lifted out of context that statement is not true! The Word only brings freedom to those who believe and seek to live it, i.e. disciples. When we believe Jesus is the exact representation of God and choose the life He is proclaiming we become disciples. Thus, He says *"If you abide in My word, you are My disciples indeed."* The English translates the next word as "and;" it would, however, be more properly translated as "then" *THEN you shall know (experience) the truth, and the truth shall make you free."*

Jesus is stating what He has said many different ways on many different occasions: Intellectually knowing the truth has never set anyone free. Experiencing the truth is what sets us free. The only people who experience the truth are disciples, because they seek to put it into practice. They desire to live in the Kingdom which is not about talk, but power. They want to live the life God intended from the beginning: to walk in love with God and man.

When the New Testament speaks of freedom it is always pointed to two factors: 1) what did we get set free from? Sin! 2) what did we get set free to do? Walk in love! Those who have no commitment to follow Jesus are like a newly paroled prisoners whose only intention is to get out and live a life of crime. Their freedom is their destruction. Those who choose to follow Jesus as Lord, use their freedom to enjoy a life better than anything they've ever dreamed: the Kingdom of God.

HeartWork

Read Every Time: The Kingdom of God is internal. HeartWork is designed to remove any internal obstacles that prevent me from entering the realm where I experience Heaven on Earth!

1. Do I read God's Word looking to know and relate to God?

2. Do I always look to Jesus when I desire to see God?

3. List the top five ways you have used your freedom in Christ?

CHAPTER 25

The Law of the Seed

You can determine what comes into your life tomorrow by the seeds you plant today!

Jesus was a preacher and teacher of the Gospel of the Kingdom. His primary means of helping people grasp the truth of the kingdom was through the use of parables. The parables made it possible for the listener to perceive how God's Word would be applied from His original intention. The parables of the Kingdom showed us the practical application of God's Word, but most importantly it showed us how to develop our hearts.

While there are exceptions, parables usually only convey one or two key points. Some, however, take on a wider dimension! Parables convey spiritual reality by comparing natural principles the listeners understands with spiritual principles he or she may not understand. Jesus talked about farming, shepherding, weddings, and other social factors which were based on simple, straightforward morals and values. If a listener had a repentant heart, the stories were readily adaptable to spiritual truth in real life application. He cut through the incredibly complicated and legalistic Jewish codes and helped people return to the Torah as God originally intended.

In His teaching Jesus employed an interesting technique where a listener hears a story, they can easily understand because it is about things with which they are familiar: farming, shepherding, weddings, weather, and other cultural and natural phenomenon. The parables are metaphorical in nature. Through this approach, the listener internally applies the principles of the story to a totally different subject. These techniques have been studied and developed in recent centuries for their incredible influence.

Most of the people, could not actually read the Bible for themselves. Therefore, their beliefs had been shaped by the religious elite to "hammer" them into submission. God's Word had not been taught as instructions for loving one another; it was taught as a way to judge one another. They knew the Word of God they simply had wrong interpretations that led to unfruitful application.

If Jesus had approached them doctrinally several negative things would have happened. The conscious mind would have reacted to argue their beliefs were right. The religious elite would have found basis for accusation against Jesus. Jesus' approach kept them from becoming defensive; they were able to open their heart and mind. Because of Jesus' use of storytelling and intimate knowledge of the Word of God, He could take people through personal transition without confrontation. He made truth simple… to those who actually wanted it! Since the parables are principle-based, every person was allowed the freedom to hear, interpret and apply from their own heart.

In the parable of the sower and the following parables of the seed, we have the key to interpreting and applying God's Word from a Kingdom perspective. But like all God's mysteries, it is hidden in plain sight, and only those who are willing become like little children can grasp their simple, but obvious, revelations of spiritual reality!

In Mark 4:13, as previously stated, Jesus reveals a master key for interpreting and applying all scripture, relating to the Kingdom. *"Do you not understand this parable? How then will you understand all the parables?"* It could be in these parables of the seed, we not only understand the Kingdom, but we may also actually possess the key for opening the door to all things!

When God created the universe, He did so around what I call absolute universal laws. In the third book in this trilogy of the Kingdom, we will explore the Law of the seed in a way that will unravel all the mysteries of faith. This will make your walk with God, people and personal development so simple! But for now, we must at least get an overview.

The physical world functions on what we call laws of physics. For God to create a physical world, He had first to conceive every law of physics. The number and the mathematical calculations for the size, weight, distance and energetic factor of all things; the temperature of all the suns in all the universe,, all the stars, their weight, size, rotation, etc, all have to be calculated in order to sustain a perfect energetic, atmospheric balance on planet earth to sustain life. Plus, the billions of cellular interaction that must happen in the physical body every second, had to be formulated by God in His own heart before He spoke them into existence.

All of creation had to be in harmony! In fact, when you see the word "good" used in the Old Testament it nearly always carries the idea of harmony. Through many of the phases of creation, God would it is good. It was good because it was in harmony. The concept of harmony as it relates to every dimension of life, faith, and the natural world seems to be lost on the entire western world. The Europeans were great at organizing, creating structure. They built empires that could last longer than any on earth. But in our expansion, it seemed harmony has never been considered. Harmony among people, races, countries, the human body and medicine, planet earth and the ecosystem has been completely ignored for the sake of financial and governmental control. Other groups were just as violent, brutal and immoral, but they were not as good at organization and control.

One of the things essential, before there could be a physical creation, was the introduction of polarity. Without polarity, the physical world could not exist. Polarity is the presence of complementary opposites. It is not about one being better than the other, it's about the fact that without both there could be no existence. Polarities provide the "field" wherein a physical world can exist, and energies can be organized to create the seen and unseen creation. Some believe the first mention of light and darkness in Genesis was actually a referral to. There was not yet any sun or moon, giving credibility to the fact that this may well be something very different than mere light and darkness. Whether that is factual or not does not, however, negate the fact that everything in this realm must have polarity to exist.

Polarity is probably the first law of creation. By it all things exist! The Ancient world would have unlikely grasp the laws of polarity. But it is worth mentioning that the ancient Chinese who originally worshipped Jehovah, and have the same account of creation and the fall of man, as the Bible, recorded in their ancient language. The idea of polarity is metaphorically addressed by many other ancient civilizations. Despite the way ignorant Europeans and Americans have vilified the concept, this is exactly what the Chinese were referring to when mentioning yin and yang. These are not some occult, religious concept. It is the Words in their language describing the two complementary forces of energy by which all things exist!

Since Jesus had no interest in sparking a philosophical debate about the science of creation, He found a better way to convey what is probably the most significant law of the universe. He taught about the seed. The law of the seed opens so many doors it is amazing; but more than anything else the law of the is the Key to the parables of the Kingdom!

The first law of the seed is every seed bears after its own kind. The first thing we discover is you can't reap what you don't sow, and you can't sow one type of seed and expect a different kind of crop to grow. This introduces a level of personal responsibility diametrically opposed to the codependent victim mentality utilized by politicians, medical professionals, and other entities seeking to take the masses captive by his own greed and laziness.

Personal responsibility is woven through all the parables of the Kingdom. Jesus' teaching and all the commandments of God. No wonder the Word of God is hated by those who seek to enslave others. When people discover they can change their world by changing what they believe they will no longer depend on corrupt leaders (con artists) for their survival. We choose what seeds we will sow in the garden of our heart, we live in that garden and partake of the fruit. No one can change that for us! It is an immutable law.

If we believe what Jesus and the entire Word of God have taught about personal responsibility, all of our social programs would be designed to help people develop a sense of personal responsibility instead of turning them into victims, with an entitlement mentality. People would be rewarded for honesty and a good work ethic. Instead, much of the church has become infected with the lawlessness, that Jesus warned would bring the destruction of our world, while giving rise to the antichrist

Another things this law of the seed teaching us is this: there is a constant exchange taking place between us and everything in existence. This concept is far more multi-dimensional than appears at first glance. But for the sake of this discussion, let's talk about the law of exchange. Polarity facilitates a continuous flux or exchange. Everything in the universe operates around these laws of exchange.

The law of the seed shows us it is impossible to receive what we do not give. Every seed bears after its own kind! Our heart is the soil, the seed is the information, true or false, that becomes a belief. Beliefs drive our emotions and behavior without any conscious effort. The parable of the sower clearly teaches the degree of thoughtful reflection, study, pondering, remembering, re-living or attention we give to anything is like tending the garden after the seed has been planted. These internal actions determine to what degree any idea we entertain will affect our lives: how much fruit it bears.

That to which we give the most attention, grows. This is why Paul says,

> *Finally, brethren, whatsoever things are true, whatsoever things are honest, whatsoever things are just, whatsoever things are pure, whatsoever things are lovely, whatsoever things are of good report; if there be any virtue, and if there be any praise, think on these things. Those things, which ye have both learned, and received, and heard, and seen in me, do: and the God of peace shall be with you.* Phil 4:8-9.

Sadly, we plant seeds of fear, unbelief, sadness, and sorrow; those are the seeds we water and fertilize through continual reflection, and we expect a little religious prayer to violate an immutable law God set in place, and miraculously give us peace. If we want peace we should follow the teachings of Paul, Jesus and God Himself in the Torah: choose life and make that the focus of our attention: i.e., magnify the Lord, instead of the problem!

God provided the simple truths in many ways throughout His Word, but Jesus explicitly taught the law of the seed as the pivotal understanding for Kingdom living. We can choose to make this law work for us, or we can, by default, have it constantly working against us. Instead of trying to use our faith to get God to give what He has already given, through Jesus, we can use our faith to believe life works by the laws He has established and operate them!

HeartWork

Read Every Time: The Kingdom of God is internal. HeartWork is designed to remove any internal obstacles that prevent me from entering the realm where I experience Heaven on Earth!

1. Do I choose what I will think about?

2. Do I realize every thought is either planting or nourishing a seed in my heart?

3. Do I think God will violate my will, and make me think differently?

4. Am I ready to start taking steps to get control of my thoughts, and begin planting the seed of life and peace in my heart?

5. You may want to consider ordering a Belief Band. Visit www.impactministries.com/product/belief-band for instructions about how to interrupt destructive thoughts by using the Belief Band.

CHAPTER 26

Heart Laws of the Kingdom

Decide if you want to be the person who lives the way Jesus teaches!

Nothing about Kingdom living is, difficult or hard to understand, unless we have rejected walking in love, as God defines it, and replaced it with other philosophies and values we trust more than we trust God's. This is what the Bible calls lawlessness, i.e. iniquity! Any time someone suggests how confusing this is, I like to point them to Mic 6:8, *"He has showed you, O man, what is good. And what does the Lord require of you? To act justly and to love mercy and to walk humbly with your God."* (NIV) Nothing complicated!

It's time we stop interpreting the parables as teaching about how to get "saved" and recognize His teaching as the Bible identifies it. He was a teacher of the Gospel of the Kingdom. The Kingdom of God is life in a realm where Jesus is Lord and we choose to surrender to Him. The Kingdom of heaven is a realm wherein all the resources of heaven are available to us. We become citizens of that realm and enjoy the benefits and resources of the King. Our only other choice is to wander in the wilderness.

We need only to identify the key beliefs and principles revealed in the parables if we want to live the Kingdom life. I refer to these as the *Heart Laws of the Kingdom*.

The Heart Laws of the Kingdom is not an exhaustive list. These are just a few of the important things that jump out at first glance. When reading and pondering God's Word, we must always ask in a teachable frame of mind, asking this question: *Father, what are you showing me in this parable that applies to my life today?*

HeartWork

1. Prayerfully review and ponder these Heart laws of the kingdom.

2. Consider whether or not your attitudes and beliefs align with these essential truths.

3. When there is disharmony between your beliefs and God's truth, reconcile that difference by aligning your heart with His.

4. In the upcoming days, weeks and months review these and incorporate them into your life and decisions.

5. Remind yourself daily, "I am seeking first the Kingdom of God and His righteousness!"

6. When you're reading begin prayerfully reading Jesus parables to discover what He will speak to your heart.

The Kingdom Of God Is Not Just Salvation

"Unless one is born again, he cannot see the Kingdom of God ."(John 3:3)

The new birth allows us to see and perceive what we could have, but not to know experientially. The Kingdom of God is a realm we enter when we trust and surrender to God's rule in our lives through the Lordship of Jesus Christ.

The Lordship Of Jesus

"If you confess with your mouth the Lord Jesus and believe in your heart that God has raised Him from the dead, you will be saved." (Rom. 10:9)

We absolutely must be surrendered to the King and the laws of His Kingdom if we want to enter His realm. The Lordship of Jesus is required for salvation (Rom. 10:9-10), which opens our eyes to perceive the Kingdom (John 3:3). Every kingdom has a king, and the King's words are law. Our laws are not laws we follow to earn the benefits of the realm; they are God's wisdom given as prescriptions for living the Kingdom life.

The Kingdom Is Internal

"The Kingdom of God does not come with observation...For indeed, the Kingdom of God is within you." (Luke 17:20-21)

147

The Kingdom cannot be perceived naturally nor by scientific observation, self-scrutiny, self-discipline, or keeping the laws.[1] Nothing external provides entrance or evidence to the Kingdom nor does it open the doors of the Kingdom. According to the parable of the sower, the Kingdom is a realm we enter when our heart receives the Word of the Kingdom, and we facilitate that seed-bearing fruit in our life.

Live By The Laws Of The Kingdom

"Not everyone who says to Me, 'Lord, Lord,' shall enter the kingdom of heaven, but he who does the will of My Father in heaven…depart from Me, you who practice lawlessness." (Matt. 7:21-23)

The laws of the Kingdom are not the rules we obey to gain entrance or to acquire improved benefits. The laws of the Kingdom are just as much universal laws as gravity, cause and effect, or entropy. These laws are not enforced by God for or against anyone but work for those who know, trust, and yield to them. The laws of the Kingdom are the commandments of God applied from the motive of love based on Jesus's example!

Those who reject or replace God's morals, values and standards with other philosophies are workers of iniquity, i.e. lawless. The harvest growing in their life is the product of the seed they have chosen to sow.

Internal Reality Determines External Manifestation

"All these evil things come from within and defile a man." (Mark 7:23)

Everything Jesus taught was about the Kingdom of God, the laws of which govern thoughts and beliefs which, in turn, direct behavior. The Hebrew word for both *heaven* and *mind* are connected. The way we think and believe produces an internal reality whereby heaven on earth is experienced no matter what the external circumstances. The words *heaven* and *mind* are also related to the word *robber* or *thief.* Our thoughts, our belief system, can rob us of heaven on earth, causing us to live in hell on earth, or facilitate heaven on earth.

The Kingdom Realm Manifests The Inheritance

"The Kingdom is righteousness, peace, and joy." (Rom. 14:17)

Righteousness is a continuum - a state of being, a power, a heartfelt perspective describing a realm wherein we abide. Righteousness is also a behavioral standard. The basic meaning of *righteousness* is *as it should be,* which describes our spiritual, emotional, physical, and behavioral state when we are as we were created to be.

The word *peace* in both the Old and New Testaments describes a tranquility

1   Theological Dictionary of the New Testament, abridged edition, Copyright © 1985 by William B. Eerdmans Publishing Company. All rights reserved.

based on the confidence that all the resources for the quality of life God offers are available. Unlike the peace the world gives, which is purely circumstantial, the peace of God is based on the resources of God. The confidence that His resources are ours is based on the quality of the relationship.

Joy is the celebration of a festive heart that is internally experiencing intimacy with God and access to all His provision. Righteousness, peace, and joy in the Holy Spirit is the fruit of Kingdom living as well as the proof!

The Kingdom, Commandments, And Covenant Do Not Conflict

"Till Heaven and earth pass away, one jot or one tittle will by no means pass from the law." (Matt. 5:18)

Jesus said:

> *Do not think that I came to destroy the Law or the Prophets. I did not come to destroy but to fulfill. For assuredly, I say to you, till heaven and earth pass away, one jot or one tittle will by no means pass from the law till all is fulfilled. Whoever therefore breaks one of the least of these commandments, and teaches men so, shall be called least in the kingdom of heaven; but whoever does and teaches them, he shall be called great in the kingdom of heaven* (Matt. 5:17-19).

The word *fulfill* does not mean *to be done away with*; it means *to be brought to its original goal or intention*. When we walk in love, we fulfill the commandments, when we use them to understand how to walk in love we fulfill them!

God never intended for the commandments to be twisted into legalistic laws used to judge one another. The commandments are God's prescription for love and, when applied from that motive and intention, the commandments define our actions. When we commit to walk in God's love, we will treat people in accordance with the commandments because we want to express God's love to others, not to appease God. The Apostle Paul said when we walk in love, we fulfill the commandments.

God is not the author of chaos and confusion. The Word of God is the Greek word *logos*, meaning every word is congruent and true only when connected to every other Word of God. People who see conflicts in the Word of God are those who have embraced the doctrines of men, poor interpretations, and personal bias. Congruence is essential because *every kingdom divided against itself is brought to desolation* (Matt. 12:25).

Jesus Is The Way, The Truth, And The Life

"I am the way, the truth, and the life. No one comes to the Father except through Me." (John 14:6)

Jesus is the way to the Kingdom and the model for the way to live in the Kingdom. His path is the path we walk. He is the truth. His life and teachings are the perfect representation of God. His interpretation and application of the commandments is the truth God always intended and is the fulfillment of Scripture. Life is in Him personally, not in doctrine about Him. We access the Resurrection life through our fellowship with Him. Any interpretation or application of Scripture not based on Jesus' life, teaching, death, burial, and resurrection is in opposition to the Lordship of Jesus.

Seek The Kingdom And Righteousness First

"Seek first the kingdom of God and His righteousness, and all these things shall be added to you." (Matt. 6:33)

While the Kingdom of God is the rule of God, the kingdom of heaven represents the provision and protection within that realm. Matthew 6:33 tells us not to worry about provision. Prayer was never intended to get things from God. All we need is available within His realm. Pray is how we commune with God, but it is also a means of exercising our authority.

Like all things to do with the heart, there is a great paradox about trusting God for provision. As a Shepherd and Father, God provides for His own. We access all the Father's resources through our relationship with Him, but to seek Him for what we can get borderlines the corrupt and evil. Realizing God as our Provider and Source is great motivation to be aware of the prize set before us, but when the desire to get exceeds the desire to live under Lordship and pursue a life lived in righteousness, it is nothing more than spiritualized greed.

The Kingdom Above All Else

"The kingdom of heaven is like a merchant seeking beautiful pearls, who, when he had found one pearl of great price, went and sold all that he had and bought it." (Matt. 13:45-46)

The way of the Kingdom is counter intuitive: **we must die to live and give to receive**. In the world, we do what we do to get the things we desire or meet our needs. We think gratifying the desires of the flesh will satisfy our longing, and this is *"... the way that seems right, but in the end leads to death."* (Pro. 14:12) We cling to our self-destructive ways to meet needs that can only truly be met in a relationship with God through our Lord Jesus Christ. Fear of losing these things keeps us from seeking the Lordship of Jesus and living in the righteousness of God; therefore, we choose to trust our carnal ways and reject faith in Jesus as Lord whom we do not trust.

Until we want God and His righteousness more than anything else, our heart cannot grasp it!

The Yoke Of Jesus

"Take My yoke upon you and learn from Me, for I am gentle and lowly in heart, and you will find rest for your souls. For My yoke is easy and My burden is light." (Matt. 11:29-30)

The concept of a *yoke* in the Hebrew mindset represented a person's doctrine - interpretation and application of Scripture. Taking Jesus' yoke means to build our life on the teachings of the Lord Jesus Christ. Our every doctrine and application of Scripture must be in harmony with what He taught and modeled.

Jesus based His life, teaching, ministry, and conduct on everything God had ever spoken as well as the meaning and the intention behind what He said. When we take on His yoke, we enter the Kingdom realm where life gets easy and light. When we hold to our own philosophies or religious ideas life is always going to be hard.

No Iniquity Of Heart

"I will declare to them, 'I never knew you; depart from Me, you who practice lawlessness." (Matt. 7:23)

We cannot grasp the Kingdom of God if we harbor iniquity or wickedness in our heart. The Old Testament makes reference to the crooked heart - a heart that is not *straight*, aligned or in harmony with God's truth. When we have a crooked, bent, broken, or wounded heart it distorts everything we hear and see. Our understanding becomes darkened and corrupted. We become incapable of finding the good God offers (Prov. 17:20).

Matthew 7:21 describes the difference between a worker of iniquity and a disciple. The disciple trusts and builds his or her house (life) on the solid foundation of God's Word, not because it is required, but because it is perceived as a wisdom greater than his or her own wisdom. The worker of iniquity rejects God's Word as the absolute truth and twists it to fit his or her personal preferences. This lack of foundation is why the house cannot stand when subjected to wind, rain, and floods. The subsequent destruction is not God's doing. The house is destroyed because of the person's own foolishness. The worker of iniquity chooses to trust his or her own wisdom more than he or she trusts God's wisdom.

The description of a true disciple is a person who builds every aspect of life, as much as can be understood, on the life and teachings, and the death, burial, and resurrection of the Lord Jesus Christ.

> *Therefore, whoever hears these sayings of Mine, and does them, I will liken him to a wise man who built his house on the rock. But everyone who hears these sayings of Mine, and does not do them, will be like a foolish man who built his house on the sand." (Matt. 7:23, 24, 26, 27)*

151

Finding The Door

"Repent, for the kingdom of heaven is at hand." (Matt. 4:17)

During 45 years of counseling and ministry, the people who would not eliminate chaos (evil) from their lives are too numerous to count. The most common default phrase for not trusting God is, *I don't understand*. The interesting truth is that when we choose to believe the Word, understanding will follow. When we choose not to believe, we will never understand the Word. The refusal to trust God's Word is most often based on the fact that it conflicts with our own thoughts and opinions. We find it difficult to envision how God's Word could come to pass in our situation; therefore, we trust and lean on the arm of flesh (our own strength).

The teachable person has a repentant heart capable of understanding the reality of the Kingdom and finding the door to that Kingdom. A repentant attitude facilitates believing, but the unrepentant and unteachable never even perceive that deliverance is near. Both John the Baptist and Jesus began their ministries with the same message: *Repent, for the Kingdom of God is at hand!* Without a repentant heart, this Kingdom cannot be seen and perceived, heard and understood. The unrepentant, unteachable never even perceive the door.

We Must Be As Children

"Assuredly, I say to you, unless you are converted and become as little children, you will by no means enter the kingdom of heaven. Therefore, whoever humbles himself as this little child is the greatest in the kingdom of heaven." (Matt. 18:3-4)

It is hard to imagine all the possibilities of what it means to become like a little child. In Greek, *little child* can mean anything from a young child to an embryo. The key factor in being a little child, however, appears to be the fact that a child is not yet fully developed and is ready to learn and be taught about all things. To become like a little child means that we must *turn*, which includes both turning *away* from something and turning *toward* something else. The main thing from which we must turn is our insistence that we understand life, God, good, and evil.

Children do not make things complicated. Complication is a form of internal resistance. If we make something hard, difficult or confusing we can pretend our intention to put them in practice will come as soon as we figure it out…. which never happens!

As humble children of God, we are teachable and ready to surrender our view and opinion to God's view and opinion. While the humble yield and align with God, the proud resist and oppose the Lord. When our hearts are full of pride, we try to feel safe by our reasoning, having success according to our logic, feel loved by our standards because we trust our way more than God's.

The little child trusts the Father for protection and provision. He has no need to understand all the complication of the world. He plays all day with the simple confidence He will be cared for.

Kingdom Is Inherited, Not Earned

"Then the King will say to those on His right hand, Come, you blessed of My Father, inherit the Kingdom prepared for you from the foundation of the world." (Matt. 25:34)

While the Kingdom is inherited and not earned (1 Cor. 6:10; Gal. 5:21; Eph. 5:5), these Scriptures clarify that we cannot inherit the Kingdom if we choose ungodly, unethical and immoral ways of life. This does not mean that God takes away from us; it means that we cannot inherit the Kingdom because we have rejected it. The Kingdom is righteousness, peace, and joy, so those who reject righteousness, reject peace and, therefore, have no joy. Choosing darkness over light brings with it the path of pain and destruction. Those who seek evil are, by default, choosing the fruit of evil, and God has no choice but to give them over to their desires.

> *Do you not know that the unrighteous will not inherit the kingdom of God? Do not be deceived. Neither fornicators, nor idolaters, nor adulterers, nor homosexuals, nor sodomites, nor thieves, nor covetous, nor drunkards, nor revilers, nor extortioners will inherit the kingdom of God. (1 Cor. 6:9-10)*

Kingdom Is A Mystery

"To you it has been given to know the mystery of the Kingdom of God." (Mark 4:11)

The Kingdom of God is a mystery, and a mystery is revealed through a series of initiations. God tells us exactly what He offers in the Kingdom and the process for accessing it. Intellectually knowing the process is not the same as making the journey. We walk with God as He leads us through learning how to apply His wisdom in this present moment, which prepares us for how to apply His wisdom in the next moment.

Once we have mastered what God wants to teach us in this moment, and we get it to work, we are ready to move to the next step. In these initiations of the heart, we do not skip steps because we feel we are too spiritual for the steps in between. Every time we get a heart revelation and true understanding, grace enables us to walk through that current aspect of truth to the next stepping-stone.

Everything Is Based On Faith

"The time is fulfilled, and the kingdom of God is at hand. Repent, and believe in the gospel." (Mark 1:15)

Every aspect of entering and living in the Kingdom is based on faith - trusting God with our heart. Without faith it is impossible to please God. Why? Faith is trust, and if we do not trust God, we consider Him to be an unfaithful liar. There can be no relationship apart from trust.

It was very easy for the Hebrew people to believe what Jesus taught about the Kingdom because they knew the Scriptures and very quickly recognized that His interpretation and application of the Word of God was truly correct. Jesus' teaching about the Kingdom bore witness in their heart because it aligned with the names of God. Not only that, but it was for the people and not against them. Jesus made God easy to trust.

Faith in God starts with faith in what God has said, most specifically what He said about Himself. Until we know what God said about Himself, we may have faith, but it is more likely to be faith in our culture, denomination, or in our opinion.

The ultimate faith is in Jesus, not that He lived, but He was who He said He was. Believing on Jesus starts with believing His representation of God, and is consummated on believing what He accomplished through His death, burial, and resurrection to such an extent that we surrender to Him as Lord.

Preach The Message Of The Kingdom

"And this gospel of the Kingdom will be preached in all the world as a witness to all the nations, and then the end will come ."(Matt. 24:14)

The Gospel of the Kingdom was the message Jesus proclaimed. The inheritance of the Kingdom was what Jesus provided through His death, burial, and resurrection.

From Eden until New Jerusalem, it was and will always be God's goal to provide a Kingdom for His children wherein all of our needs are met, and we experience continual fellowship with God and one another. The Gospel of the Kingdom reveals every step of that plan beginning with Jesus revealing God to the world, to His crucifixion and resurrection, obtaining and sharing the inheritance, the need for godly living, and finally His Second Coming. The absence of the Kingdom message is responsible for the absence of disciples, which explains an impotent church that fails to reach the world and struggles with personal victory.

The Seed grows by itself

"The kingdom of God is as if a man should scatter seed on the ground, and should sleep by night and rise by day, and the seed should sprout and grow, he himself does not know how." (Mark 4:26-27)

The soil is the heart; our responsibility is to tend the soil and plant the seed. The seed does not grow because we have all the answers or the perfect doctrine. The fruit that grows in our life is the product of two simple factors: the kind of seed we plant and whether or not we work the soil.

Pondering, considering, and meditating on the Word we receive, is like working the soil and watering the plant. We cannot make seeds grow nor can we make them grow any faster. We can only plant and then tend to the seed and the soil.

The Law Of Personal Responsibility

"Each of us shall give account of himself to God." (Rom. 14:12)

Through many of the Kingdom parables, a conclusion emerges without words ever being spoken: personal responsibility. We are all free-will agents who make our own personal choices and, therefore, must live with the consequences of those choices. Our personal responsibility is in stark contradiction to pop psychology, humanism, and socialism which have become the predominant basis for rejection of God's personal Word.

Scripture leads us to believe every human being has the law of God written in the deepest part of their being, and even legitimate testing shows that we all have capacity for the same moral compass. The way of the wicked, however, is to want others to be responsible for our bad behavior. This prevalent iniquity will be the destruction of civilization as we know it; it will give rise to the man of iniquity, *the antichrist*, and it will take the world to the brink of destruction. The world will only be saved by the personal return of the Lord Jesus Christ, who will establish Kingdom rule for one thousand years, before the final rebellion and the establishment of New Jerusalem here on earth!

The first law of the seed is this: every seed bears after its own kind! This is the ultimate expression of personal responsibility. I choose what kind of seed I will plant in my heart by what I listen to and allow myself to see. Human beings are created in the likeness and image of God. We are the only species that has the ability to change the direction and the quality of our life by making choices.

CHAPTER 27

Exercising Authority

People with authority make decisions and take action!

We, the body of Christ, are a nation of priests and kings, we are members of the eternal royal family. We have access to the all the resources of heaven By nature of our family, we have a realm of authority that is unparalleled in the earth. While it is passionately proclaimed in demonstrative sermons, it is seldom understood, believed or put into practice. One would think, the promise of personal authority would inspire a world wide-revival. In fact, there should be one of the most phenomenal mass transformations of believers to occur in the history of the church. If believers actually began to operate in personal authority there should be an unprecedented outbreak of miracles, healings, and even financial breakthroughs. But even more impressive to the world that hates the church, they could finally see a church walking in love the way God intended, because we would overcome our personal issues. But... that's not happening. Why?

Unlike the religious leaders of His day, Jesus taught as one having authority, Mk. 1:22. His connection and confidence in God were sure, unwavering, and unshakable; therefore He was confident, sure, unwavering and unshakable. Unlike the theoretical teaching of religionists, Jesus' teaching and subsequent actions produced quantifiable results. Instead of people walking away feeling confused, condemned and more burdened, they walked away with answers, insights, but most importantly: solutions. His disciples wanted a connection with God that produced the same results in their lives. After all, a disciple seeks to live as the master lives, and Jesus lived as a man with authority.

Authority is often confused with power. The loss of the distinction renders the believer powerless, unsure and afraid to act. Power is the strength or energy that makes something happen, but *authority* is the right to use that power. God's Word violently departs from religion in this significant way: power belongs to God, but here on planet earth, authority has been delegated to mankind!

The first two laws of man's identity are these: 1) we are the likeness and image of God, and 2) we have dominion in planet earth (Gen. 1:26). The Psalmist says it like this: *The heaven, even the heavens, are the Lord's; But the earth He has given to the children of men*, Ps.115:16. It would seem that neither God nor the devil can do anything in earth apart from human beings who use their authority to make it so.

Luciferian doctrine also denies that Jesus came as a real man.

Luciferian doctrine ignores man's authority on earth, thereby creating a *strawman* argument against God. Based on erroneous concepts of sovereignty, the argument against God is as follows: since the Creator is in control of everything, He is obviously evil; otherwise, we would not have war, murder, and oppression on earth. This Luciferian concept has subtly woven its way into the doctrinal fabric of mainstream Christianity to intentionally subterfuge the character and nature of God, with the ultimate purpose of undermining our authority. As long as we succumb to Luciferian concepts of Sovereignty, we never know when to take action. We are constantly waiting on God to do what He has actually already done through the Lord Jesus.

The logical derivative of this doctrine is to blame God for all the evil in the world. Since God is responsible, we are not responsible. If we have no responsibility, we have no authority. Modern psychiatry, along with all forms of humanistic and socialist philosophy, always makes others responsible for the actions of the and consequences of the individual. And yet, the silver thread of personal responsibility woven throughout Jesus' teaching stands diametrically opposed to God being in control of our fate. It is we who are to use our God-given authority over our lives, temptations, and desires.

Man's irrational willingness to buy into the false Sovereignty doctrine may well be because it pacifies one of our most carnal human tendencies: rejection of personal responsibility. Our deep-rooted insecurities and low self-worth drives us to always look for someone or something outside ourselves to blame for our problems. We reject the first law of the seed. Every seed bears after its own kind. In other words, I am living the beliefs which are the fruit of the seeds I have planted in my heart!

We sometimes forget that while Jesus worked powerful and persuasive miracles, an equally powerful and persuasive testimony to His faith was His personal character, integrity, ethics, morality and emotional stability. The disciples had seen

Jesus challenge the money changers in the temple, face threats against His life, and incur vicious slander from the religious leaders, yet He still lived in peace and walked in love. Most amazingly, He stayed on course with God's purpose for His life. His message and His life were in complete congruence.

Considering the obvious hypocrisy of the religious rulers, witnessing One with such power and authority but who was not corrupt or self-righteous, had to be a persuasive testimony for Jesus' followers and a glaring indictment against those who accused Him. The disciples witnessed that Jesus first used His authority over His own life, temptations, and struggles, which led to authority in His ministry.

At some point, the disciples wanted what Jesus had. They knew power belonged to God, so they, like us had to wonder, "How do I function in God's power with the same confidence Jesus' displays?" They, evidently, knew Jesus authority came as a result of His personal connection to God. For that reason, they finally came to Him and asked, *"Teach us to pray..."* Today, people would think the capacity for Jesus' level of authority must be the result of a special anointing. Immediately, the Gnostic doctrine that has been taught as Christian, would have led them on the endless pursuit of the illusive anointing, i.e. something they would never find.

The Hebrew believer had no vain illusions of personal anointing or access to God's resources apart from a personal connection and relationship with God. Seeking God's resources without first knowing God is hypocritical. The disciples knew power belonged to God. Like the prophets of old, those who flowed in personal power were those who remained intimately connected to God. Prayer, meditation, communion and the Word was the only way of life for a committed believer. Every true follower of God knew life revolved around walking with God, which, from the beginning, was a matter of the heart, not legalistic observance of the commandments. The true follower of God wanted to understand how Jesus connected with God and how that manifested in such dynamic personal authority.

The various Hebrew and Greek words for prayer each point to different types of prayer. But the core understanding of the Hebrew word for *pray* means *to assess and reconcile* or *assess and decide*.[1] This type of biblically based prayer only occurs from a person who understands authority. Jesus referenced this exact definition both times He used the term *bind and loose*. Binding and loosing is an execution of authority. The believer takes action based on God's Word and what Jesus accomplished at the cross.

Binding and loosing in Matthew 16:19 is better understood from the Amplified translation *"...and whatever you bind (declare to be improper and unlawful) on earth must be what is already bound in heaven; and whatever you loose (declare*

---

1   Theological Wordbook of the Old Testament. Copyright © 1980 by The Moody Bible Institute of Chicago.

lawful) on earth must be what is already loosed in heaven." We must know what God says to be true, what God has clearly stated as His will, and specifically what Jesus accomplished in His death, burial, and resurrection. That is God's will; there's nothing to ask, nothing to pray about. To pray or ask God if something accomplished through the cross is HI swill is a declaration of our unbelief in the finished work!

In Jesus, we are free from all the curse of the law (Gal. 3:13), and we have an inheritance of all the promises God has ever made to anyone (2 Cor. 1:20). This is powerful information, is the basis upon which we take our rightful authority. Religion has taught us to ignore what God has declared legal or illegal through the death and resurrection of Jesus, which is tantamount to rejecting His finished work. Instead of using the authority God has given to establish His will in our life, we ask God to use His authority. Yet, the opposite is true: God provides the power when we act on the authority He gave us. Authority activates His power, and we have been given authority in Christ.

Why did Jesus never pray and seek God's will before casting out demons or healing the sick? Simple! He knew who God was and trusted in His name. Jesus knew He had the right as well as the responsibility to act on God's Word and His name. We are also responsible for manifesting God to the world, which we do by acting on His revealed will for mankind.

Jesus teaching did not introduce new doctrine; he clarified what God said in Deuteronomy 30:15,19: *"I have set before you life (good) and death (evil), blessing and cursing; therefore choose life."* He made it abundantly clear: when faced with the challenges of life or death, good or evil, we do not need to pray for God to act; we need to make a choice. Choosing is more than merely desiring; it is substantiated with intention and followed by commitment.

In Romans 10:6-8, Paul repeats what Moses said thousands of years earlier, which is a concept very nearly lost on the modern believer:

> *For this commandment which I command you today is not too mysterious for you, nor is it far off. It is not in heaven, that you should say, 'Who will ascend into heaven for us and bring it to us, that we may hear it and do it?' Nor is it beyond the sea, that you should say, 'Who will go over the sea for us and bring it to us, that we may hear it and do it?' But the word is very near you, in your mouth and in your heart, that you may do it (Deut. 30:11-14).*

Even under the Old Covenant, there was nothing to pray about, no big mystery regarding what God wants for us. It is simply a choice when you trust and believe what God has already said. How much more can we be sure of God's will in the New Covenant than the resurrection of Jesus? We do not need a new revelation; we do not require someone to bring or explain God's will to us. By trusting in God's Word, character and nature and believing who we are in Christ, we are

Dr. Jim Richards

empowered to act with inherent authority - right to choose - which has been given to all mankind by our Creator!

In Matthew 16:19, Jesus reveals His secret of personal authority: use the keys of the Kingdom to open the doors to all that is yours in Christ. This is what He meant by binding and loosing. Jesus has provided for every area of lack we experience; therefore, we must *loose* it into our present experience. We must declare what is legal in our lives according to the will of God that is declared legal by the resurrection. We must call it forth and command it to be so! Likewise, anything from which Jesus set us free through the cross, we must *bind* and declare illegal. We must command it to depart. There is nothing to wonder regarding the will of God nor is there anything else that needs to be done other than what Jesus has already done!

Apart from expressing and manifesting our personal authority through binding and loosing as the Keys of the Kingdom, we will never experience what has been freely given. We will know about the Kingdom, but we will be hindered by every opposing factor. Binding and loosing are how we execute our authority by assessing what is occurring in our life. If we determine it is not in harmony with what Jesus has provided, through the cross, we must reconcile it.

God cannot and will not violate your will, or freedom of choice. The truth only sets us free when we apply it. If you know and believe what God has done for us in Jesus, it is left to you to use your authority and change the curse into the blessing. God will provide the power when you make apply the truth!

HeartWork

Read Every Time: The Kingdom of God is internal. HeartWork is designed to remove any internal obstacles that prevent me from entering the realm where I experience Heaven on Earth!

1. Do I find myself wavering when faced with a situation that needs to be overcome?

2. Do I find myself asking God to take authority when I should be taking authority?

3. Do I trust that God will manifest His power when I express my authority?

4. Create a personal meditation of yourself facing a storm, with fierce wind and rain. Use your imagination to see, hear, and experience it as completely real. Then, imagine yourself speaking to the storm. As you stand waiting, feel the confidence and assurance that what YOU say comes to pass. Then notice the wind and rain decreasing. Imagine the sound of the rain becoming softer and softer until it has all stopped and become completely peaceful. Do this exercise every night as you are drifting off to sleep for at least a month.

5. If you are interested in developing your heart to be immovable in your trust for God, click here to learn more about our Heart Physics program: www.HeartPhsyics.com.

CHAPTER 28

Moving From Knowledge to Application

The truth presented in this book is not hidden, nor is it complicated! For those who believe on Jesus as Lord, it is not burdensome.

1. Jesus came to bring us the abundant life, Jn 10:10.

2. That abundant life is the by-product of personal, intimate, experiential knowledge of God, and the Lord Jesus, Jn 17:3.

3. Being born again is not the only prerequisite for this abundant life, but it does open the eyes of my heart to the possibility of experiencing this life, Jn. 3:3.

4. I can live as a carnal Christian which is modeled by the Israelites wandering in the wilderness, or I can trust God and follow Him into the Kingdom, which was depicted in the Israelites who believed God and entered into Canaan, 1 Cor 10:6-11, Heb 4:1-2.

5. The Kingdom cannot be seen outwardly, Lk. 17:20,

6. The Kingdom can only be entered internally, Lk. 17:21.

7. To live in the Kingdom, I must be surrendered to the King, Ro. 10:9-10,

8. There are Keys to the Kingdom, Matt 16:19.

9. The keys are based on personal authority, Matt. 16:19

10. It is our responsibility to establish the Kingdom in our lives through binding and loosing, Matt. 16:19.

Heaven on Earth is the first in a trilogy, This volume serves to unveil the mystery of the Kingdom of God, showing you, the believer, the simplicity of entering a realm called the Kingdom of God.

Now that you know what Jesus taught about the Kingdom the next step is to apply this information, based on Jesus teaching. In Volume Two *Heaven on Earth: The Secret of the Keys of The Kingdom* I will remove the religious influences that have made authority seem far away and difficult by showing you the simplicity of operating in personal authority!

Jesus is our Lord, our example and our teacher. When we remove the religious mysticism, His teaching becomes abundantly clear, Get ready to see Jesus in an entirely new light that will change the way you see and experience yourself. For the first time, by Jesus' own words and example, you will know exactly how to establish God's will in your life!

Please visit www.impactministries.com/heavenonearth to order your copy of *Heaven on Earth: The Secret of the Keys of The Kingdom.*

ABOUT THE AUTHOR

In 1972, Dr. James B. Richards accepted Christ and answered the call to ministry. His dramatic conversion and passion to help hurting people launched him onto the streets of Huntsville, Alabama. Early on in his mission to reach teenagers and drug abusers, his ministry quickly grew into a home church that eventually led to the birth of Impact Ministries.

Prior to his salvation, Jim was a professional musician with all the trappings of a worldly lifestyle. More than anything, he was searching for true freedom. Sick of himself and his empty pursuits, he hated all that his life had become. He turned to drugs as a means of escape and relief. Although he was desperate to find God, his emotional outrage made people afraid to tell him about Jesus. As he searched for help, he only became more confused and hopeless than ever.

After listening to his bass player grumbling about a verse of Scripture that a Christian had shared with him, Jim had a miraculous encounter with God. From this one Scripture he was able to experience God's love! He gave his life to the Lord and was set free from his addictions. His whole life changed! Now, after years of ministry, Jim still believes there's no one that God cannot help, and there's no one God does not love. He has committed his life to helping people experience that love. If his life is a model for anything, it is that God never quits on anyone.

With doctorates in theology, human behavior and alternative medicine, and an honorary doctorate in world evangelism, Jim has received certified training as a detox specialist and drug counselor. His uncompromising, yet positive, approach to the gospel strengthens, instructs and challenges people to new levels of victory, power and service. Jim's extensive experience in working with substance abuse, codependency and other social/emotional issues has led him to pioneer effective, creative, Bible-based approaches to ministry that meet the needs of today's world.

Most importantly, Jim believes that people need to be made whole by experiencing God's unconditional love. His messages are simple, practical and powerful. His passion is to change the way the world sees God so that people can experience a relationship with Him through Jesus.

Jim and his wife, Brenda, have six daughters, 15 grandchildren, and continue to reside in Huntsville, Alabama.

For additional content and resources please visit this book's companion webpage: http://www.impactministries.com/heavenonearth